DISCRETIONARY EQUALITY

Equal Opportunity, 1954–1982

by

Joseph King Jr., EdD

ISBN: 978-1-4269-5620-1 (sc)
ISBN: 978-1-4269-5621-8 (e)

Library of Congress Control Number: 2011903903

Trafford rev. 03/17/2011

 www.trafford.com

North America & International
toll-free: 1 888 232 4444 (USA & Canada)
phone: 250 383 6864 ♦ fax: 812 355 4082

ACKNOWLEDGMENT

The writer wishes to express his graditude for inspiration and support given by Mrs. Jessie and Joseph King Sr., Ethel and John Nix, the Nix, Dukes and King families and all family, friends and associates in and under the canopy of heaven.

TABLE OF CONTENTS

LIST OF FIGURES

Figure

ABSTRACT

This research study traces the history of the school desegregation enforcement efforts of the Education Department, Office for Civil Rights (ED-OCR). These enforcement efforts in ED are investigated and assessed. The study begins with a background discussion of the historical factors leading to the inconsistent application of equal educational policy.

Very shortly after the old Department of Health, Education, and Welfare was established in 1953, a significant court decision, *Brown v. Board of Education*, ordered the desegregation of the nation's schools. From the *Brown* decision in 1954 to 1981, equal education policy was inconsistently enforced at the national level. The causal factors of inconsistent educational policy and enforcement are rooted in many complex social and political forces. As the Education Department's enforcement effort is reviewed, social and political forces are identified and documented.

The controversial issue of affirmative action is reviewed to highlight the additional problems which impaired policy enforcement. The development and status of current affirmative action procedures are discussed and reviewed. The legislation in the Congress which has developed since the enactment of the Civil Rights Act of 1964 is discussed.

The politics of federal policy is also discussed. The chapters cite presidential leadership, congressional initiative, and the effects of political interest groups as factors which influence the lack of uniformity of policy and enforcement due to politics.

Lastly, the study identifies the consequences of the Department's inconsistency, addresses the concept of discretionary equality, and argues that the implementation of equal educational opportunity warrants the uniformity of equal educational policy and enforcement. The last chapter provides a summary, and the current status of compliance is assessed. Due to many complex political issues, activities, and social forces, the enforcement of equal access in education continues to be wrought with controversy, indecision, and slow progress.

The study identifies those unique factors and argues for coordination of efforts to effectively implement equal educational opportunity. This coordination of effort involves the branches of government and agencies collaborating with and assisting one another in developing simultaneous policies and compliance practices which will eliminate other social problems while effectively promoting equal opportunity in education.

CHAPTER I

INTRODUCTION: POLITICS OF EQUAL EDUCATIONAL OPPORTUNITY

When I first became interested in the issues presented in this study, I felt the U.S. Department of Education's enforcement of equal education policy was plagued with deliberate "footdragging." I envisioned an "evil motive" in policy enforcement. Even though the data reveal some deliberate footdragging, additional data reveal the complex role of politics and highlight activities of the Executive branch, the Congress, and interest groups.

Educational policy h as been inconsistently enforced at the national level. The U.S. Education Department's equal education enforcement effort from 1954 to 1981 will be investigated and assessed in this study. The thrust of this study is the administration of policy grounded in an interpretation of legal issues.

The reason why educational policy was inconsistently enforced is primarily due to politics. Politics, as defined in the study will identify competition between and among competing interest groups or individuals for power and leadership. Politics is viewed from the national level; the President's leadership is reviewed to document the scope of direction on these matters. Congressional initiative is discussed to reveal the impact the legislative branch has on administration of various departments and agencies in the federal government. Interest group activity is also reviewed.

Politics is discussed in terms of function (i.e., the effects of political interests on the function of government in society). Often, matters relating to federal policy decisions can be made by judges. The policy making of judges is especially common in constitutional matters; therefore, significant court decisions play a major role in equal education issues at the national level.

Chapter One, "Introduction: The Politics of Equal Educational Opportunity," serves as a background to the remainder of the study. The chapter discusses the *Brown v. Board of Education* decision and other significant court cases. A discussion of social forces and civil rights reflects the efforts which brought about the civil rights legislation that promotes equal educational opportunity. A discussion of educational inequality focuses issues in education which raise controversial questions regarding equal educational opportunity. These issues give rise to competition among interest groups for influence in educational policy enforcement. The historical factors identified have led to the inconsistent enforcement of educational policy at the national level.

Chapters Two through Five identify factors which influence inconsistent policy enforcement. Chapters Six and Seven explain inconsistent policy enforcement due to politics (e.g., competition between and among competing interest groups or individuals for power and leadership). Chapter Eight presents the argument that "to implement equal educational opportunity the uniformity of educational policy, and enforcement is warranted." Chapter Eight also identifies the major consequences of the government's inconsistencies. The major consequences are: (1) an ineffective school desegregation enforcement from 1954 to 1981, (2) the lack of full implementation of the 1954 *Brown* decision, (3) a failure to implement the Civil Rights Act of 1964, specifically Titles IV and VI.

I. THE PROMISE OF *BROWN*

The promise of *Brown* concerns the faith and hope many people have for the celebrated *Brown v. Board of Education* decision that mandates equal education. The promise of *Brown* is discussed as a historical factor which set the stage for the Supreme Court's viewing of equal educational opportunity issues. The position of this writer is that twenty-eight years after the *Brown* decision, the legal provisions of the decision have not been implemented. The chapter starts by describing the letter and spirit of the decision. Current issues and court cases are discussed to corroborate the intent of the *Brown* decision in 1954.

The *Brown* decision signaled a conscious effort on the part of the Federal Government, in particular the judicial branch, to remedy past inequities. At the time of the decision in 1954, it was believed that education was the most significant vehicle for social mobility and, in particular, integration. The ruling in *Brown* signaled a breakthrough in the monolithic pattern of discrimination and prejudice. At the time of the *Brown* decision, the black church and college were the most important institutions in black America. These institutions mutually enhanced each other by promoting education in the church and religion in the colleges. Due to the deeds of philanthropy by whites, most black colleges found their beginnings supported by white religious and social organizations (Bullock, 1967).

In *Brown v. The Board of Education of Topeka, Kansas 347 U.S. 483 (1954)*, the opinion consolidated similar cases presented to the court prior to 1953. The decision also set the foundation for legal aspects of equal education policy. The opinion had far-reaching implications for educational opportunity and supported a broad interpretation of law.

> Brown was a consolidated opinion covering cases arising in four states: Kansas, Delaware, Virginia, and South Carolina. A common issue justified their consideration together and resulted in a ruling which held that compelled segregation of students by race is a deprivation of the equal protection of the laws as guaranteed by the 14th Amendment. Although the holding in *Brown* clearly was directed against legally sanctioned segregation, language in *Brown* supported a broader interpretation. The Court expressly recognized the inherent inequality of all segregation noting only that the sanction of law gave it greater effect. (U.S. Comm. on Civil Rights, 1975, p. 31)

The language in the *Brown* decision supported a broad interpretation of prohibited segregation of students by race. Even though the ruling was clearly directed against legally sanctioned segregation, the broad interpretation recognized inequality of all segregation. The *Brown* decision came down in two distinct parts, *Brown I* and *Brown II*. *Brown I* focused the segregation question, and *Brown II* the corrective action necessary to enforce a right. *Brown II* (*Brown v. Board of Education, Topeka, Kansas, 347 U.S. 294 [1955]*) came essentially after the question of remedy was before the Supreme Court. The finding in *Brown I* exposed the dual public school system operating in Topeka, Kansas. The Court's opinion noted two types of segregation, *de jure* and *de facto*. *De jure* segregation is the official and deliberate separation of students based on race.

Many states operated these dual systems under state laws which sanctioned such activity. *De facto* segregation is the separation of students without any; official authority. The separation comes about inadvertently or accidentally. Many of these *de facto* systems operated in the north and west. Although the *de facto* systems were not illegal, the opinion in *Brown* required school districts to put forth a "good faith" effort to establish a uniform public education system. The "good faith" effort was emphasized to assist states in developing a uniform public education system. The catchwords in the *Brown* case, "with all deliberate speed," were emphasized in the opinion to exemplify the pace of change envisioned by the Supreme Court.

The decision in *Brown v. Board of Education* was "one of the great milestones in the history of the United States" (Berry and Muse, 1964, p. 1). From the years 1954 to 1964, the Federal Government's efforts to eliminate discrimination were nil. In 1964 a significant effort come about on behalf of the Federal Government to regulate anti-discrimination cases in the public interest. The developments in the period 1954 to 1964 were initiated by Black plaintiffs determined to assert their rights under the law. The *Brown* decision gave many black Americans hope for a new period of opportunity and equal justice under the law, In 1981, the spirit of *Brown* was currently visible; the charge has been taken by many groups to overcome past inequities. The *Adams v. Richardson* court case, which will be discussed in the next chapter, reveals the efforts taken by groups to overcome past inequities in education.

Just as efforts continue to implement the *Brown* decision, efforts to change the focus of viewing these educational matters are present. Two distinct court rulings in the *Bakke* and *Weber* cases apply to affirmative action in education and employment. The *Bakke* and *Weber* cases will be thoroughly discussed in a subsequent chapter. However, as late as July 3, 1980, the Supreme Court ruled that the Congress (only) can set racial quotas.

The ruling applied only to an act of Congress, which the Court said has unique powers. Educational institutions, governments, government agencies, state legislatures, and others gained little more guidance than they had under the court's earlier *Bakke* and *Weber* affirmative-action rulings. It also provided a license for the future. Within certain broad limits, the Court said, Congress may favor a minority group whenever it makes a finding of past discrimination and tailors its racial preferences to correct that discrimination. The findings need not be specific or rigorous as is required when a judge imposes a remedy. And the Court said that people who lose out in such programs—generally whites—need not have been found guilty of discrimination themselves. (*Washington Post*, July 3, 1980)

Opponents and proponents of the decision, however, agreed in one area: they all said it has far-reaching implications beyond federal contracting. It can be applied to housing, employment, education and any area that Congress feels people have been discriminated against in the past and need a remedy. (*Washington Post*, July 13, 1980, p. 1)

Since the issues in the *Bakke* and *Weber* affirmative action rulings, the Supreme Court has been consistent on its remedial action decisions in discrimination matters.

Supreme Court Chief Justice Warren in 1954 delivered the *Brown* opinion:

Today, education is perhaps the most important function of state and local governments. Compulsory school attendance laws and the great expenditures for education both demonstrate our recognition of the importance of education to our democratic society. It is required in the performance of our most basic public responsibilities, even service in the armed forces. It is the very foundation of good citizenship. Today it is a principal instrument in awakening the child to cultural values, in preparing him for later professional training, and in helping him adjust normally to his environment. In these days, it is doubtful that any child may reasonably be expected to succeed in life if he is denied the opportunity of an education. Such an opportunity, where the state has undertaken to provide it, is a right which must be made available to all on equal terms.

To separate ... [children] from others of similar age and qualifications solely because of their races generates a feeling of inferiority as to their status in the community that may affect their hearts and minds in ways unlikely to be undone.... Whatever may have been the extent of psychological knowledge at the time of *Plessy v. Ferguson*, this finding is amply supported by modern authority. Any language in *Plessy v. Ferguson* contrary to this finding is rejected.

We conclude that in the field of public education the doctrine of "separate but equal" has no place. Separate educational facilities are inherently unequal. Therefore, we hold that the plaintiffs and others similarly situated for whom the actions have been brought are, by reason of the segregation complained of, deprived of the equal protection of the law guaranteed by the Fourteenth Amendment. (Brown v. Board of Education, 347 U.S. 483 [1954]

The above statements reflect the court's views on the significance of equal education in society and outlaw the doctrine of "separate but equal."

Other recent court decisions have affirmed the legal principles contained in the Brown decision. Even in *Bakke* the major emphasis in *Brown* has gone unchanged. The Burger court in rendering that decision made a major shift from the Federal Government leadership role in these matters by referring many such matters to courts of lesser authority (Institute for Southern Studies, 1979, p. 31).

In *Bakke*, Justice Brennan's opinion reads,

At least since *Green v. County School Board* ... it has been clear that a public body which has itself been adjudged to have engaged in racial discrimination cannot bring itself into compliance with the Equal Protection Clause simply by ending its unlawful acts and adopting a neutral stance. Three years later, *Swann v. Charlotte-Mecklenburg Board of Education* reiterated that racially neutral remedies for past discrimination were inadequate where consequences of past discriminatory acts influence or control present decisions.

And the court further held ... that courts could enter desegregation orders which assigned students and faculty by references to race.... Moreover, we stated that school boards, even in the absence of a judicial finding of past discrimination, could voluntarily adopt plans which assigned students with the end of creating racial pluralism by establishing fixed ratios of black and white students in each school. *Green* ... was recognized as a compelling social goal justifying the overt use of race. (Regents of the University of California v. Bakke, 1978)

The reaffirmation of many legal principles is inherent in the body of the *Bakke* decision. Mr. Justice Marshall, the only Black Supreme Court Justice, emphasizes the legal history of Negroes (Blacks) in their constant struggle for equality. In the concurring opinion in Bakke, Justice Marshall states,

Most importantly, had the Court been willing in 1896, in *Plessy v. Ferguson*, to hold that the Equal Protection Clause forbids differences in treatment based on race, we would not be faced with this dilemma in 1978. We must remember, however, that the principle that the "Constitution is color-blind" appeared only in the opinion of the lone dissenter (163 U.S. at 550).

The majority of the Court rejected the principle of color-blindness, and then for the next 60 years, from *Plessy* to *Brown v. Board of Education*, ours was a nation where, by law, an individual could be given "special" treatment based on the color of his skin.

It is because of a legacy of unequal treatment that we now must permit the institutions of this society to give consideration to race in making decisions about who will hold the positions of influence, affluence, and prestige in America. For far too long if we ever become a fully integrated society, one in which the color of a person's skin will not determine the opportunities available to him or her, we must be willing to take steps to open those doors. I do not believe that anyone can truly look into America's past and still find that a remedy for the effects of past discrimination is impermissible. (Regents of the University of California v. Bakke, 1978, p. 15)

The previous statements highlight the fact that a remedy for unlawful discrimination is permissible. The thrust of the *Brown* decision and the power of the position are features which have affected subsequent decisions. Justice Marshall highlights the ruling in the *Brown* case in light of his previously stated decision in *Bakke*.

Reassertion of the
Principles of Brown

Just as efforts have been made to reassert the legal principles in *Brown*, many efforts to forestall and render the decision insignificant have developed. McCord (1969) states the necessary import of *Brown* and its predecessors is that Blacks cannot obtain equal educational opportunity within the Constitution where within an educational environment children, white and black, are taught separately. McCord (1969) points out that the decision has been misinterpreted in some instances. Instead of expanding the reading and interpretation, the courts have sometimes limited the reading and interpretation.

> In *Briggs v. Elliott*, one of the original cases involved in the *Brown* opinion,
> Judge Parker dwelt upon what *Brown I* did not expressly say. On the grounds
> that the Constitution has an impact of negation only, Judge Parker concluded
> indicating that "the Constitution ... does not require integration. It merely
> forbids discrimination." This interpretation was quickly taken up by a host of
> federal courts. (Briggs v. Elliott, 132 F.Supp. 76 [E.D.S.C. 1955] id. at 77; Kelly
> v. Board of Education, 270 Fed 209. 228-29 [6th Circuit 1959])

These statements are important in that they reveal a different interpretation from the one given in *Brown*. As stated, this interpretation was taken up by a host of federal courts.

Briggs goes far to ignore the consideration of segregation, unless it is presently mandated by statute; but it fails to give weight to the notion of injury from segregation. Additionally, *Briggs* disregards the legal rights of Blacks to obtain equal educational opportunity.

> Today the *Briggs* analysis of negation is moribund and all but totally discredited.
> It has been rejected by the Fifth, and Third, the Eighth, and the Tenth Circuits,
> and by district courts in the District of Columbia. (Hobson v. Hansen, 269
> F.Supp. 401 [D.D.C. 1967])

The above ideas reassert the fact that the decision in *Briggs* has been discredited.

The initial response of lower courts to *Brown II* was to require "freedom of choice" desegregation plans on a grade-a-year basis. By the end of 1958, every state with segregated schools (*de jure*) adopted some form of law authorizing school closings to avoid desegregation.

Four states completely prohibited expenditure of state funds for desegregated education. Eight states supported substitution of racially exclusive (white) private schools for desegregated public schools, and five states authorized transfer of public school property to private schools. Ultimately, all eleven states with school systems segregated by law at the time of *Brown* repealed or modified compulsory attendance laws, and six states weakened or eliminated teacher tenure provisions. (U.S. Senate, S. Res. 359, February 19, 1970)

The above statements are a brief description of the action some states took to subvert the *Brown* decision. The massive resistance movement was an effort by many opponents of the *Brown* decision to overturn the ruling. The efforts by the groups were titled "massive resistance." Despite the decline of the massive resistance movement, there has been a futile attempt on the part of the federal government to desegregate the public schools.

As the first decade after *Brown* drew to a close in the spring of 1964, only 2.25 percent of Negro children in the eleven southern states attended school with whites, and faculty desegregation was practically nonexistent. (U.S. Senate, S. Res. 359, February 19, 1970)

The above ideas cited in the Senate document in 1970 reveal the poor state of compliance with the decision ten years after it was rendered.

Prior to 1964 there was no established Federal enforcement role in school desegregation cases. President Eisenhower did intervene to protect the rights of Blacks in Little Rock's Central High School. In Little Rock, the state government refused to uphold the Federal court order of integration. The weight of governmental authority fell with particular force upon the National Association for the Advancement of Colored People (NAACP), which had taken a leading role in the *Brown* case and subsequent efforts to enforce its mandate. In five states, legislative committees conducted widely publicized investigations of subversive and un-American influences in the NAACP specifically and the civil rights movement generally. Other committees probed the NAACP for evidence of criminal law violations and tax evasions. Statutes designed to prevent the organization from supporting desegregation suits poured out of state legislatures. Existing laws regulating out-of-state corporations and taxes applied tax exemptions harshly in the case of the Association. Governors were granted emergency powers to halt organizational activity. State officials demanded that NAACP membership lists be made available for public inspection. State employees were required to list membership in the NAACP—grounds for dismissal for state employment (U.S. Senate, S. Res. 359, February 19, 1970, p. 194).

When the government did get involved in school desegregation after the ten-year lapse from 1954 to 1964, much of the effort addressed practices in southern school systems, while the north was left alone. Some believe this emphasis was placed on the south due to political reasons. Orfield (1969) notes that political opposition to forced desegregation began to swing into full stride during the 1968 election campaigns, when George Wallace and Richard Nixon, in their competition for southern votes, criticized HEW and the courts for going too far and extolled the virtues of freedom of choice. When Nixon took office, HEW's desegregation efforts came to a standstill "in the rural and urban South as well as in the northern cities." Eventually Nixon's public position on desegregation and busing would be even more conservative than that of the southern governors (Middleton, 1979, p. 35).

President Nixon's school desegregation policy included the granting of money to schools under the Emergency School Aid Act (ESAA) to schools implementing school desegregation policies. There was no monitoring of these funds by HEW, and many school districts were in the process of not complying with any of the civil rights laws. This is discussed in the *Adams* litigation in the next chapter.

According to Orfield (1978), most statistics show that "substantially higher levels of segregation" remain under court-ordered plans than under HEW-negotiated plans. Additionally, data suggest that there is less white flight in HEW-negotiated plans than in court-order plans.

The Lack of Commitment to Brown

In light of *Brown*, many commentators have suggested that there has been an eroding commitment in the equality of educational opportunity. Initiatives were introduced in the Congress for constitutional amendments and legislation to limit the authority of the Federal courts and agencies to remedy unlawful segregation in schools (e.g., the Eagleton-Biden Amendment). Much of the debate around the issues of educational opportunity focused on misleading issues such as "busing" and "racial balance" and on issues that effect the promise of educational opportunity. These issues have caused great controversy and an eroding commitment.

Federal courts, and Federal agencies under the Civil Rights Act of 1964, act only to remedy segregation imposed by the discriminatory acts of public authorities. Even then, they do not require any "racial balance" in the schools. (U.S. Senate, December 31, 1972, p. 188)

Generally the emphasis on racial balance comes from the development of a desegregation plan designed to work. The "busing" issue is quite controversial in that groups that oppose it complain of excessive transportation.

> According to HEW's 1970 school survey, 42 percent of all American public school students are transported to their schools by buses; an additional 25 percent ride public transportation.
>
> HEW estimates that only 3 percent of all public schools use busing for the purpose of desegregation.
>
> Department of Transportation attributes less than 1 percent of the annual increase in student transportation to school desegregation. Transportation of students is so common in school districts throughout the nation that there can be no legitimate reason to forbid its use as one tool in remedying discrimination. In most, if not all, cases, transportation has been held within reasonable limits. In the 23 largest school districts undergoing desegregation in the fall of 1971, the Department of HEW estimates that the proportion of students transported rose only 7.5 percent. (U.S. Senate, December 31, 1972, p. 189)

The above ideas reveal the actual statistics regarding student transportation in the fall of 1971. At that time, most if not all transportation was held within reasonable limits. The issues of busing and racial balance further offset the emphasis in *Brown*. Parents are often confused due to the controversy around the issues. Many parents feel "busing" will result in the transportation of their children to inferior schools. Parents also feel that the problems in newly desegregated schools may escalate due to "community resistance" and intra-school problems. In many communities, parents have overtly protested in front of the desegregated school building. For example, New Orleans, 1960:

> During the last days of November 1960, Reverend Lloyd Foreman and Mrs. James Gabrielle, who had continued to take their children to the Frantz school after one Negro girl began attending, were subjected to abuse and physical violence by the mob in front of the school. This coupled with the fact that several parents in the Frantz school area had appealed to S.O.S. for help in returning their children to school, led to the organization of a volunteer "carlift" run by parents from the uptown section of New Orleans, which transported the children to school in relative safety. (Institute for Southern Studies, 1979, p. 63)

Brown and Equal Educational
Opportunity

The spirit of *Brown* addressed the educational needs of the "disadvantaged" child in that "separate was not equal." The issues in 1981 take us away from the true intent of the Supreme Court's decision. Prior to *Brown*, the original founder of the NAACP (DuBois, 1935) wrote on education and asserted:

> Theoretically, the Negro needs neither segregated schools nor mixed schools. What he needs is Education. What he must remember is that there is no magic, either in mixed schools or in segregated schools. A mixed school with poor and unsympathetic teachers, hostile opinion, and no teaching concerning black folk, is bad. A segregated school with ignorant placeholders, inadequate equipment, poor salaries, and wretched housing is equally bad. Other things being equal, the mixed school is the broader, more natural basis for the education of all youth. It gives wider contacts; it inspires greater self-confidence and suppresses the inferiority complex. But other things seldom are equal, and in that case, Sympathy, Knowledge, and the Truth outweigh all that the mixed school. (p. 335)

This emphasis by DuBbois parallels the elements of the *Brown* case that address the spirit of educational opportunity.

Jones (1978) summarizes the changing mood in America as one of eroding commitment. Jones contends that in America today there is an assault on policies and programs in education that have been designed to help the poor, Blacks, minorities, and women:

> There is also an assault on the concept that a proper role of the federal government
> is to intervene in the lives of individuals and groups so as to move individual and
> group life in the direction of the American Creed. (p. 258)

According to Jones, the eroding commitment is evident in education, and the changing mood in America does not address equal educational opportunity.

Other commentators have discussed educational opportunity and highlighted the elements of the *Brown* decision that have a unique relationship to blacks and education.

Gunnar Myrdal wrote the *American Dilemma* (1944, 1962). He assessed the social problems in American society and called the situation an American dilemma.

Myrdal's key points were:

1. Negroes' statutory right to public education has remained unassailable, even in the south, where it is probable that face-saving was necessary because of the American Creed. Without it, and without the influence of the Negro school and college, the Negro would have been driven back to slavery, for all intents and purposes, in the reactionary periods.

2. The persistent support of northern philanthropy was a key factor in maintaining Negroes.

3. The implications of classical versus vocational education as appropriate to Negroes are important in terms of the motives of the whites in power as well as in terms of the attitudes of Negroes themselves.

Myrdal held that the American Creed prescribes that Negro children should have as much educational opportunity as anyone else in the same community and that Negroes should receive the kind of education which would make them good and equal citizens in a democracy which values culture (Jones, 1978, p. 269).

Myrdal's analysis of the American Creed dictates that Blacks should receive every educational opportunity for social mobility. Not unlike other ethnic groups who travel to the United States for opportunity and social mobility, the American Black has also sought education for social mobility. Myrdal (1944, 1962) studied this very issue and concluded that America has reiterated the unique value of education as a right and a vehicle for social mobility.

Myrdal contends:

> At least since the time of Horace Mann, Americans have been leading in the development of pedagogical thinking. The marriage between philosophy and pedagogy in Dewey and his followers has given American the most perfected educational theory developed in modern times. Under the slogan "education sociology," it requires that education be set in relation to the society in which the individual lives. The introduction of this value relation into discussions of educational goals and means is a paramount contribution of America. And this has remained not only an achievement of academic speculation and research but has, to a large extent, come to influence policy-making agencies in the educational field. (Myrdal, 1962, p. 883)

These statements point out the leadership role Americans have played in education. Educational sociology issues and discussions of educational goals have influenced policy-making agencies. The American Creed, according to Myrdal, dictates that Negro (Myrdal's language) youth should have as much educational opportunity as any other group. Formal education has a vital role to play in that it will increase the forces for raising the status of the Negro; for example:

1. More formal education means more assimilation of the majority culture, thereby decreasing dissimilarity of Negroes from other Americans [Myrdal's language].
2. Formal education trains and helps give Negroes an economic livelihood, so that they are ready to move into new positions when opportunities arise.
3. It is a means of social mobility, and since large numbers of Negroes are in the lower classes, education presents the possibility that the entire class will climb in status.
4. Increased formal education will make the Negro more dissatisfied with his 1 changes the Negro's traditional charade of response patterns, which are outmoded in today's world (e.g., docility and passivity).
7. Formal education provides a means of self-realization for the Negro, thereby enhancing his ego and belief in himself.
8. Leaders are developed through the educational sorting and selection process. (Jones, 1978, p. 251)

Jones (1978) also contends that these events of formal training not only develop Black Americans but have implications for white Americans. White Americans can dispel previously stereotyped notions about Black inferiority, if whites relate to black people wanting to learn and better their conditions. The implications for Blacks are that the race can uplift itself socially through formal education.

The suggestions continue, although in light of *Brown*, parallel concepts address the same and similar issues which focus on educational opportunity. Not only have white Americans championed the significance of education for blacks, but Blacks have held education as a high priority.

> As self-improvement through business or social improvement through
> government appears so much less possible for them, Negroes have come to affix
> an even stronger trust in the magic of education. (Myrdal, 1962, p. 884)

This statement highlights the quest blacks have had for educational opportunity. Not unlike other ethnic groups, black Americans, too, put hopes and aspirations in education. In *Up from Slavery*, Booker T. Washington (1902) wrote:

Few people who were not right in the midst of the scene can form any
exact idea of the intense desire which the people of my race showed for education.
It was a whole race trying to go to school. (p. 29)

It is clear that Blacks and whites have shown great interest in education in the United
States; and those results of schooling, as they are viewed, motivate and interest groups of all
races. These principles attached to schooling in the United States symbolically address the *Brown*
decision's emphasis on equality of educational opportunity. Not unlike Booker T. Washington,
W. E. B. Dubois expressed in *Soul of Black Folks* (1903) the significance of the "joy" Blacks
felt after emancipation and the problems of the Black schools. DuBois talked about the special
contribution blacks make to society and that their intellectual pursuits cannot be denied. He
promotes a libertarian approach to education which would "help free" the minds of Black folk.
This approach Dubois took in 1903 is alive today in the promise of *Brown*.

The promise of *Brown* is identified as a historical factor that led to the Department
of Education's inconsistent application of policy. Current issues and cases were discussed to
corroborate the intent of the *Brown* decision as it is currently viewed by some.

II. SIGNIFICANT COURT DECISIONS AND LEGISLATION

In addition to the *Brown* decision, other significant court cases and legislation are
historical factors that led to and explain inconsistent policy enforcement. The cases represent
actions by groups and individuals for power and leadership in education policy formulation.

Other significant court cases have directed the judicial branch's involvement in equal
educational opportunity. In 1969, in *Alexander v. Holmes County Board of Education, 396 U.S.
1218 (1969)*, the Supreme Court intervened to decide a case where the Justice Department
sought a delay due to litigation. The Court held that school systems are constitutionally required
(under the 14th and 15th Amendments) to desegregate first and litigate later. The Supreme
Court's opinion in *Alexander* conflicted with the Department of Justice policy that sought a
delay in desegregation while the school board was involve din litigating the desegregation matter.
In this matter the Supreme Court charted the government's position.

Under President Richard Nixon's administration, the chief executive prescribed a less
effective enforcement effort in school desegregation cases. Whereas the HEW Office for Civil
Rights had procedures to conduct Federal fund cutoffs prior to litigation, President Nixon
prescribed the Department of Justice to litigate prior to any Federal fund cutoff. On March

24, 1970, President Nixon made a statement which warned that desegregation must not be disruptive. In his statement the President emphasized the neighborhood school concept that limited desegregation plans to the school closest to t he child's home. On August 3, 1971, the President stated that he "consistently opposed busing to achieve racial balance" and that he was opposed to the busing of children for the sake of busing (Statement by the President, white House Press Release, August 3, 1971). In that same statement, the Presidentinstructed the Attorney General and the Secretary of HEW to limit busing to the minimum legal requirement by law.

Later, the Supreme Court in *Swan v. Charlotte-Mecklenburg Board of Education 402 U.S. (1971)* emphasized that busing was "a normal and accepted tool of educational policy." Furthermore, it emphasized that desegregation plans could not be limited to the neighborhood school. Prior to *Swann*, desegregation plans were limited to the school closest to the child. Proponents of this concept felt their choice of housing was influenced by the neighborhood school. *Swann's* significance outlined additional techniques in eliminating discrimination. "A frank—and sometimes drastic—gerrymandering of school districts and attendance zones, resulting in zones

> ... neither compact nor contiguous, indeed they may be on opposite ends of the city ... pairing, clustering, or grouping of schools with attendance assignments made deliberately to accomplish the transfer of Negro students out of formerly segregated Negro schools and transfer of white students to formerly all-Negro schools.

Swann signaled innovative approaches and techniques to remedy city-wide segregation.

In *Keyes v. School District No. 1, Denver, Colorado, 413 U.S. 189 (1973)*, the Supreme Court ruled that absent a state law forbidding integration, the school system in fact was operating a *de jure* system by its actions. *Keyes* was the first significant case decided in the north. Justice Brennan's opinion in *Keyes* asserted that the Denver school system:

> ... has never been operated under constitutional or statutory provision that mandated or permitted racial segregation in public education. Rather, the gravamen of this action is that respondent School Board alone, by use of various techniques such as the manipulation of student attendance zones, school site selection and a neighborhood school policy, created or maintained racially or ethnically (or both racially and ethnically) segregated schools throughout the

school district, entitling petitioners to a decree directing desegregation of the entire school district. (413 U.S. 189 [1973])

Keyes (Denver case) proved to be the most significant ruling against a northern school district. Whereas many northern school systems operated *de facto* systems which were proved unlawful, *Keyes* found that absent state statutes proscribing segregation, the Denver school system was operating a *de jure* system by its actions. Again, this was the first such ruling against a northern school system.

Another case which addressed issues of northern metropolitan desegregation is *Milliken v. Bradley, 42 U.S.L.W. 5249 (U.S. July 25, 1974)*. *Milliken* reaffirmed many constitutional premises in earlier cases. However, the evidence in the case did not support a finding of the lower court requiring metropolitan desegregation. The lower court ruled that the actions of the suburban school districts and the state had an effect upon the discrimination found in the Detroit public school system. For the first time, Detroit's problems presented the Supreme Court with the issue of metropolitan desegregation. Justice Thurgood Marshall stated the prime question in the case "was the area necessary to eliminate root and branch" the effects of the state-imposedand supported segregation and desegregation of the Detroit public schools (42 U.S.L. 5258).

Justice Marshall further stated,

Indeed, by limiting the District Court to a Detroit only remedy and allowing ... flight to the suburbs to succeed, the Court today allows the State to profit from its own wrong and to perpetuate for years to come the separation of the races it achieved in the past by purposeful state action. (42 U.S.L. 5277)

The significance of *Milliken* is that it suggests future developments. The Court upheld that the evidence did not support a finding of discrimination in school districts affected by the proposed desegregation plan. Another case mentioned earlier, *Bakke v. Regents of the University of California, 438 U.S. 265 (1978)*, presents the current thrust of the judicial branch on these matters.

In *Bakke* the concept of affirmative action was discussed. Affirmative action is a remedy employed to correct past discrimination. In *Bakke*,

The concept of affirmative action in the United States was in its inception designed to award preference to Blacks and other minorities in employment and education. The beneficiaries of affirmative action are the victims of past and present discrimination. Visualized as a remedial tool, the concept is a method for redress. (Reid, 1978, p. 4)

These statements highlight the concept of affirmative action and discuss the concept as a method for redress.

In *Bakke* the challenge was against the student admissions policy at the Medical School of the University of California. Allen Bakke, a white male, asserted that he was "reversely discriminated against" due to the application of the university's policy. The admissions policy set aside 16 of 100 places for economically disadvantaged minorities. The California Supreme Court upheld Bakke's allegations that the program favoring minorities at the expense of qualified whites was "reverse discrimination." The U.S. Supreme Court affirmed the California Supreme Court's decision, but emphasized the legitimacy of affirmative action. The Supreme Court ruled that the quota system at the University of California was unlawful and suggested that the University review the Harvard University affirmative action plan.

The U.S. Commission on Civil Rights is an oversight agency which reports periodically to the President and the Congress on civil rights matters. The U.S. Commission on Civil Rights implied a direct relationship between governmental action and urban-suburban segregation was to be found in the nation's public schools (1974). The previous discussion of relevant court decisions revealed a profile of the three branches of government which addressed the social problem of school desegregation. The *Brown* case represented the judicial branch approach. The President's actions during these times reflected the executive office's focus and initiative. The differences between the opinions of the Supreme Court and the executive branch's initiatives document the lack of consistency and coordination of the Federal Government to speak with one voice on the issue of school desegregation.

The Congress, in its enactment of legislation broad and sweeping in perspective and approach, documented a "new-era" of "equal opportunity" in America in 1964. The Federal Government was not the sole implementor of this revolutionary social change in America. Other social and political forces effected change and demanded the government's response. The "March on Washington" demonstrated that ethnic groups and members of the majority society could press the Congress into enacting major legislation to further secure the civil rights already vested in the Constitution.

III. SOCIAL FORCES AND CIVIL RIGHTS

Social forces and civil rights highlights historical factors which led to current inconsistent educational policy enforcement. This section identifies political elements prior to the enactment of the civil rights legislation.

Social events pressed the Congress in the enactment of the Civil Rights Act of 1964. Titles IV and VI of the Act served as a mandate for change in equal education policy. The social events leading to the Civil Rights Act can be described by the following passage which compares the civil rights movement to other social movements:

> For the first time in the long and turbulent history of the nation, almost one thousand cities were engulfed in civil turmoil, with violence trembling just below the surface. Reminiscent of the French Revolution of 1789, the streets had become a battleground; just as they had become the battleground in the 1830's of England's tumultuous Chartist movement. (King, 1963, p. 16)

The above statements compare the civil rights movement to the events of the French Revolution of 1789 and the Chartist movement of 1830. In the early 1960s, the protest for civil rights by Blacks and other disadvantaged minorities proved historically significant as the Federal Government addressed issues of civil rights protesters. Although there were concerted efforts, these efforts were not without opposition. The opposition took forms which will be discussed. The civil rights movement in the United States was primarily non-violent. A proponent of the non-violent civil rights movement, Dr. Martin Luther King, expressed the impact of this movement as follows:

> Just as lightning makes no sound until it strikes, the Negro Revolution generated quietly. But when it struck the revealing flash of its power had the impact of its sincerity and fervor displayed a force of frightening intensity. Three hundred years of humiliation, abuse and deprivation cannot be expected to find a voice in a whisper. The storm clouds did not release a "gentle rain from heaven," but a whirlwind, which has not yet spent its force or attatined its full momentum. (King, 1963, p. 16)

Dr. King's statements describe the intensity of the non-violent civil rights movement and explain the impact of these social forces.

Issues surrounding school desegregation were key concerns among activists. In 1954, the Supreme Court ordered school desegregation "with all deliberate speed." In 1963, nine years later, the catchwords "with all deliberate speed" had not become a reality. Other concerns, such as employment and housing, were voiced by protesters. Too much despair emanated from a dream deferred, the dream being equal opportunity in America's institutions and entry into the mainstream of American life. Disenchantment with the American political scene also produced reactions from protesters. President John Kennedy's administration promoted civil rights' interests. During his presidential campaign, Kennedy declared that civil rights would be a chief interest of his administration. In 1963, although two years into his term, many Black Americans felt a growing discontent with Kennedy's lack of progress in civil rights. This lack of expeditious effort reflects dimly on the Chief Executive during the times.

In employment, the quest for well-paying jobs escalated. Blacks migrated north seeking enhanced employment opportunities due to automation and industrialization. Many Blacks found themselves unprepared for the newly developed skilled trades; therefore, once again, as in the south, menial jobs were their only avenue to employment.

During the early 1960s, many students on college campuses began to demonstrate for civil rights. These demonstrations took various forms—sit-ins, picketing, and marches. The Student Nonviolent Coordinating Committee (SNCC), founded by Dr. Martin Luther King, began to organize voter registration drives, freedom rides, and other forms of mobilization activities to effect social change in civil rights. There were five major organizations involved in civil rights activities: the National Association for the Advancement of Colored People (NAACP), the Congress of Racial Equality (CORE), the Urban League, SNCC, and the Southern Christian Leadership Conference (SCLC). In April of 1960, Dr. King led a series of demonstrations in Birmingham, Alabama. For many years this southern city had been considered a "hotbed" of prejudice and blatant, comprehensive discrimination. Segregation in Birmingham in 1968 was the "catch of the day." In the years prior to 1960, Ku Klux Klan cross burnings and bombings were on the rise. The demonstrators in Birmingham were met with staunch resistance and severe police brutality. These events were highly publicized by the media with photos of men, women, and children brutally beaten while attempting to assert their rights.

> Now wave after wave of Negroes poured in the Birmingham streets and were repressed by police with spectacular brutality. Many were injured; over 3,000 were arrested. (Muse, 1968, p. 5)

These statements reveal that many blacks were injured and arrested while protesting in Birmingham, Alabama.

These events pressed the Congress to enact the civil rights legislation and subsequent Federal enforcement of equal opportunity issues. While the trouble in Birmingham escalated, many other American cities erupted with civil rights activities. Jackson, Mississippi, and Tuscaloosa, Alabama, became hotbeds of civil rights' activity. On June 11, 1963, efforts of Black students to enter the University of Alabama at Tuscaloosa were met with resistance. Alabama Governor George Wallace physically blocked the doors of the University and refused admittance to the two Black students. President Kennedy "federalized" the Alabama National Guard and gave orders to the governor to remove himself.

On June 12, 1963, Medgar Evers, a field secretary for the NAACP, was assassinated while returned home from a civil rights rally in Jackson, Mississippi. As the news media covered these events, tensions grew, and Black life in the south became increasingly more complex day by day.

During this year of protest, violence, and demonstrations across the nation, the Federal Government began to take action. Many thought 1963 to be a year of celebration. It marked the one hundredth anniversary of the Emancipation Proclamation, the 1863 document issued by President Abraham Lincoln which freed the slaves. After more than a century of slavery, 1863 indeed was a year of celebration. However, in comparison with 1963, given the conditions of the times, there was not much to celebrate. In fact, the dreams of emancipation for Blacks were seriously deferred. One hundred years later, President John Kennedy proposed a different approach to solving race problems in the country.

On June 19 President Kennedy submitted his program to Congress. It called for: (1) a ban on the exclusion of any person on account of his race from hotels, restaurants, stores, place of amusement, or other facilities; (2) authority for the Attorney General to file suits to speed desegregation of public schools and colleges when those affected could not afford to do so or feared reprisals; (3) a statutory basis for the President's Committee on Equal Employment Opportunity; (4) a ban on discrimination in all federally assisted programs and activities, with authority to withhold federal funds in cases of violation; and (5) the establishment of a Community Relations Service to help communities through disputes and difficulties in the elimination of racial discrimination. The President also urged prompt action on the proposals he had submitted earlier. "Enactment of the Civil Rights Act of 1963 at this session of Congress," he said, "—however long it may take and however troublesome it may be—is imperative." The package overshadowed all other business of the Congress during most of the ensuing year. It was modified and amended many times, and strengthened, before emerging as the Civil Rights Act of 1964. (Muse, 1968, p. 7)

The above statements highlight President Kennedy's view of the importance of the enactment of the Civil Rights Act as a prime piece of legislation during the 1963 Congressional year.

This presidential response generated substantial reaction by many people both white and Black. Prior to the enactment of the Civil Rights Act, many events occurred during the end of

1963. As interest groups became disenchanted with the "snail's pace" progress of the Civil Rights bill in Congressional committees, efforts to pressure the Congress were afoot.

A massive march was planned to pressure the Congress into enacting the civil rights bill. Again, this march as called the "March on Washington," which took place in Washington, D.C., on August 28, 1963, at the Washington Monument. The "March on Washington" was led by John Lewis (SNCC), Whitney Young, Jr. (National Urban League), Asa Philip Randolph (Brotherhood of Sleeping Car Porters [AFL-CIO]) Martin Luther King (SCLC), James Farmer (CORE), and Roy Wilkins (NAACP). This demonstration, more than any march for civil rights, proved effective. The march assisted in bringing about the enactment of the Civil Rights Act of 1964. The march showed a great sign of public interest.

IV. EDUCATIONAL INEQUALITY

Various issues relating to equal educational opportunity have been debated following the *Brown* decision. This section will discuss the areas of debate among competing interest groups and individuals in defining equal educational opportunity and its corollary terms, educational inequality. These issues discussed have been taken into account by bureaucrats in policy formulation and decision making. Current issues will be discussed to highlight and reveal the current lack of consistent government policy enforcement with regard to equal educational opportunity.

Educational inequality is defined as a disparity of distribution of educational opportunity. Given the disparate distribution as evidenced by *Brown*, the effective implementation of equal opportunity in education is currently warranted. While the civil rights movement continued its momentum, scholars and bureaucrats in the office of Education and other concerned parties began to ask the question: What is equal education opportunity? As the question was approached from different perspectives, the following gives a discussion of some of those views. Controversy and conflict have stimulated the arguments.

There has been controversy over intelligence as it relates to race. Much discussion has centered around intelligence and race. In educational circles, the question of intelligence is usually raised in conjunction with "educational opportunity" issues. Arthur Jensen is the chief proponent of a theory which hypothesizes that there are inherited differences in intelligence among races (*Bias in Mental Testing*, 1978; *Washington Post*, April 20, 1980, p. 1). With the rising interest in civil rights in the early 1960s, many Black Americans began to question test bias. It was felt that "tests" which determined life chances for Blacks had some inherent bias which precludes passage for Blacks and minorities. These "tests," which determined access to employment and educational opportunities, seemed in practice to "screen out" minorities.

The search for a "culturally fair" test continues. When data reveal that a high percentage of Blacks fail bar examinations, Law School Admission Tests, Graduate Record Examinations, and a host of other certification examinations, one might wonder why blacks and minorities are underrepresented in the test outcomes. In *Bias in Mental Testing* by Arthur Jensen, the study investigated the question: "Are mental tests in general, and I.Q. tests in particular, culturally biased so as to discriminate unfairly against racial and ethnic minorities or persons of low socio-economic status?" (*Washington Post*, April 20, 1980, p. 1). Jensen found that commonly there was a 15-point discrepancy in I.Q. between whites and Blacks. He attributed these differences to genetic inheritance.

Jensen identifies a phenomenon labeled the "general cognitive development lag," which cannot be effected by environmental influence or intervention. This philosophy implies that blacks and minorities are less intelligent than whites and that the differences cannot be changed. Jensen's works have created some controversy.

A study by James Coleman was met with controversy and conflict. James S. Coleman of Johns Hopkins University conducted and headed the second largest social science research project in history, which was mandated by Congress in 1964. The report, labeled the Coleman Study, was actually titled "The Report on Equality of Educational Opportunity." The Coleman study supports a finding of the social class of a school's student body as directly impacting race and educational equality. If an acceptance of Coleman's findings on social class variables suggests that black and minority youths would have higher achievement scores if given equal access to schools that reflect a middle-class milieu.

The U.S. Commission on Civil Rights Report makes a significant distinction between integration and desegregation as used in Coleman's study. The Coleman data imply that integration is preferable to simple desegregation. It is preferable due to educational attainment and interpersonal relations. The following passage described one situation:

> In schools which can truly be described as integrated, most teachers report no racial tension whatsoever, and Negro students evince higher verbal achievement, more definite college plans, and more positive racial attitudes than comparable Negro students in tense, merely "desegregated" schools. (U.S. Comm. on Civil Rights, 1968, p. 90)

This statement reveals the success of a truly integrated school and highlights variables of effective schooling.

Many minorities do not share the view that integrated schools are more effective. Pettigrew states, "Desegregation, then, is a necessary but not sufficient condition for integration involves in addition to racial mix a climate of interracial acceptance" (1968, p. 75).

Mere access is not fulfilling the spirit of "quality" education, nor does it reveal the spirit of the law symbolized in the *Brown* decision—educational equality among school systems. Elimination of unlawful dual systems which represent inequality, i.e., curriculum, pupil expenditure, and ineffectual instruction, is an approach to desegregation that has its roots in the *Brown* decision. It is implicit in the opinion. Any perspective that shifts from equal educational access to a different view of "quality" is not the intended interpretation of the framers of the Brown decision. The concept of integration as a goal absent quality education (racial acceptance) violates the spirit of the *Brown* decision.

The policy of compensatory education is another view of equal educational opportunity. In 1965, Congress passed the Elementary and Secondary Education Act (ESEA). Title I of this act provided an unprecedented amount of funds for improving the equality of education in segregated schools. On its face, the act was to provide programs that would compensate for differences in students who lack academic skills.

The Elementary and Secondary Education Act (ESEA) has sparked much controversy because the concept of compensatory education implies segregation. Some scholars hold the view that the school should not be the only vehicle for social equity and mobilization of Blacks and minorities, although schools do play a major role in a student's socialization and future career development.

Since Title I of the ESEA directs funds toward minority youngsters, the program tends to be segregated. Cohen (1968) asserts the segregated approach to compensatory education is limited. Cohen's primary objection is that evidence has been found to support the view that integrated schooling does assist blacks in overcoming the disadvantages of segregated schooling (Cohen, 1968). However, Cohen maintains there is no evidence to support the view that segregated compensatory education can assist in overcoming the disadvantages of segregated schooling. Again, the popular notion in Cohen's work and the primary objection to segregated compensatory education is the notion of interracial acceptance. Interracial acceptance has been tied to performance; studies have revealed that both races, Black and white, do perform well when conditions of acceptance prevail (Pettigrew, 1968).

From a national policy enforcement perspective, it is difficult to obtain compliance in terms of interracial acceptance in the classroom. To clarify this further, a national educational policy that maintains school desegregation and compensatory programs to eliminate prior educational disadvantages cannot face compliance with interracial acceptance. This kind of policy enforcement is not the intent of Congress. There are a number of ways the Federal

Government can support efforts to assist in the development of in-school programs which eliminate segregation and perpetuate a climate of coexistence and mutual understanding. The task is too great to expect the Congress or the Supreme Court to legislate or rule on moral issues; and interracial acceptance implies approval, consent, and admittance. Programmatic assistance from the Federal Government can provide research and development grants to conduct training of school personnel to develop behavioral dynamics and teach human relations skills. Some grant funding by the National Institute for Education has been provided for this purpose.

A second objection to compensatory education programs is that educational outcomes are not restricted to the development of academic competence. Given this understanding, one may question the interracial acceptance notion in regard to the nonexistence of compensatory education programs. Would interracial acceptance exacerbate absent compensatory education programs? How can we pursue goals of equality of educational opportunity without providing programs which seek to assist disadvantaged minorities in achieving educational objectives?

Cohen (1968) maintains that "a policy of segregated compensation cannot provide that binding tie and, therefore, can promise only the continuance of a segregated, closed and inferior system of education for Negro Americans" (p. 114). With desegregation as the aim, the concept of integration as it relates to interracial acceptance cannot be fulfilled. Compensatory education has been documented as successful under the Title I ESEA program.

In view of legislative options and policy alternatives, change is greatly needed in our educational systems. Many researchers studying the problem of educational inequality fail to develop innovative methods of providing educational excellence for black and minority youth. Compensatory education programs can be viewed skeptically, although policies are directed at changing educational practices (e.g., implementation). These programs can have, and sometimes do have, implications on segregation and resegregation. Given that scholastic achievement in most public schools is declining, it would stand to reason that non-minority children could benefit from these programs.

Traditionally, psychological prejudices have misguided the effects of these programs.

Examples are theories of "cultural deprivation" and related beliefs that the culturally determined, educational inferiority of Negro children will impair the ability of white children to learn if they are taught in the same classes. It is assumed that because of their background, Negro children and their parents are poorly motivated for academic achievement and will not only be unable to compete with white children but will also retard the white children. (Clark, 1968, p. 175)

Clark's interpretation of cultural deprivation theory has not led to the development of instructionally effective schools for society's children. Rather, it has perpetuated the current system, which is inefficient and advantageous to the status quo. One could suspect that a society as sophisticated as the United States would have developed an education system whose goal was designed to increase the overall development of its students. The nation's schools fulfilled the hopes of many European immigrants. The public school was a vehicle for social mobility. With the elimination of dual educational systems and integration, a steady stream of social mobility was manifested.

Alternatives to the present system are needed. Since 1940, concepts on the history of education shifted from "democracy in education" to "equity in education." In the middle of this shift is "equality of educational opportunity," which addresses the concept of educational inequality. Such a shift is warranted, although from an equity perspective it seems to eliminate and dismiss the equal educational opportunity concept.

The equity in education movement stresses academic excellence (achievement) and extends the concept of educational access. The movement focuses on what happens after equity is achieved with attention to the processes of education. It accepts equal educational opportunity as a precondition for equity in education.

As previously mentioned, the full and proper implementation of current educational policy, Title I ESEA, and HEW's equal educational opportunity policy, the goals of the equity movement could have been achieved earlier. However, these compensatory programs were stated only for the disadvantaged student, and they were considered inferior. Compensatory education coupled with the cultural deprivation theory contains an implied assumption that the "disadvantages" (e.g., environmental deficits) Black children bring to school interfere with their ability to be educated in a homogeneous setting. This view supports and obscures the inherent problems of educational inequality and sustains and perpetuates white flight from urban environs to the suburbs.

Clark (1967) proposes educational competition for the public schools through the following regional state schools financed by the states, cutting across urban and suburban boundaries.

Federal Region Schools – financed with state and Federal aid and transcending state lines with provisions for residential students.

College and University Open Schools – financed by colleges and universities to serve as educational laboratories.

Industrial Demonstration Schools – financed by business and industry to serve the children of its members and select public school pupils. The overall goal is to exemplify a model of a good comprehensive high school.

Labor Union Schools – financed by labor unions to serve the children of its members.

Army Schools – Traditionally, these schools have serviced a significant population who would have limited opportunity absent this educational resource.

The above propositions identify various alternatives which can be used to enhance educational competition (Clark, 1968, p. 186).

Predictions have indicated that competition in education is an upcoming trend. With the formation of the new Department of Education in place, teacher unions are not currently at odds. Business and industry are becoming involved in setting up staff development and training programs. McDonalds, a national corporation, is noted for its training center, "Hamburger University." Harold Hodgkinson views another type of educational competition:

> By 1984, 200 major corporations will have their own universities "colleges" or "centers" in which they will sponsor their own educational programs, not only in technical fields, but in writing, mathematics, art appreciation, and American history.... The American Association for Post-secondary Education, begun as an umbrella group in 1971, is beginning to succeed in pulling together a coalition composed of colleges, universities, industry, and the military who are concerned about the assessment and improvement of human adult performance. (Hodgkinson, 1979, p. 134)

In 1979 Hodgkinson took an approach similar to concepts expressed by Clark in 1968. Perhaps the goals and objectives of education can be obtained by giving full consideration to equity issues and equality of educational opportunity.

A legal interpretation also identifies equal educational opportunity as more than access. In essence, the state owes a greater responsibility to all of its school children than it presently accepts. It is constitutionally obliged not merely to open its door to all comers, but to provide "effective" equality to all. A reconsideration of effective equality in light of recent and extensive educational research studies, such as the Coleman Report, suggests that the state's obligation to provide an equal education is satisfied only if each child, no matter what his social background, has an equal chance for an equal educational outcome, regardless of disparities in cost or effort that the state is obliged to make in order to overcome such differences. This notion of effective education has not been emphasized by the government, educators, or parents. Equity issues (e.g., back to basics, high achievement scores, etc.) that relate to, and are implied in, equal opportunity notions have been separated. There has been a failure to address these issues and educate the public to these unique distinctions.

The Coleman Report suggests that if equality of opportunity is to be defined by "those elements that are effective for learning" (p. 20), the Court's focus school child should not be primarily on school facilities, but rather on the equalization of human resources for these resources most critically determine the fate of the individual school child (Kirp, 1968).

Thus, one might have a different perception of the concept of equality of educational opportunity based on the interpretation of the Coleman Report or the *Brown* decision. The interpretation of each places different demands on schoolsystems. Another view which sustains the Coleman argument, to focus on "effective equal opportunity," does not, imply that everyone has a "constitutional right" to perform at the same scholastic level, or to earn an equal share of A grades, teachers' commendations, or to be admitted to Harvard. Students are not all equally intelligent; they vary in aptitude and ability (Stodolsky and Lesser, 1967, p. 587).

The legal interpretation of "effective equal opportunity" goes further. It appeals to fundamental rights underlying the "effective utilization" standard. When educational opportunity laws are compared with other laws that affect rights, the utilization of the fundamental right must be granted. "This 'effective utilization' standard varies: the state is obliged to provide effective access to the criminal process; to assure the right to vote; to secure an equal chance for an equal educational outcome" (Kirp, 1968, p. 156). This statement describes one view of the effective utilization standard.

Other contrasting views dismiss educational equality as being of an significant need in society. Upon understanding that no two things are purely equal, the dimensions and scope of equality change. Some scholars believe inequalities in life cannot be rationalized with a theory of equal opportunity. Realizing that Blacks get unequal portions of educational resources, Jencks (1972), in *Inequality*, maintains,

The amount of time people spend in school is more equal than most of their other experiences. Blacks get 10 percent less schooling than whites, for example, even though their parents make a third less money. (p. 22)

This statement describes Jenck's view of the lack of educational resources and income of blacks. In addition, Jencks also maintains that if schools are free, that there is no way society can equalize consumption of educational resources. Jencks suggests alternative ways of financing education and eliminating public schools. His idea is for children interested in learning to benefit from association with their middle-class peers. Those youngsters not interested in education per se should not be compelled to go to school but provided subsidized alternatives. Jencks supports the view that, when a student decides he is not benefiting from school and quits, he should not be compelled to remain but alternative resources should become available (e.g., jobs, apprentice programs, etc.).

Jenck's philosophy raises many questions. Are schools instructionally effective for the urban poor? Can they become instructionally effective? Can an education do more to sustain a child's interests in school? Educational inequality theories have many dimensions. Duberman (1976), in *Social Inequality*, states that educational inequality is a matter of social class and not race. Given the drive of parents to transfer wealth and position to their offspring and the contrasting desire of "equality," which attempts to offer each individual opportunity, society is left with the dilemma of "mass" versus class education.

> From the time that this ideology became accepted dogma, it was conceded that not all children were equally prepared for higher education. Headstart programs were begun for very young children and "open enrollment" programs were offered in many colleges and universities, usually with remedial courses available to students who could not demonstrate adequate ability in rudimentary skills. (Duberman, 1976, p. 205)

The above statements highlight Duberman's view of social inequality and the reaction of schools, colleges, and universities to inequality. Educational inequality also entails the issues of testing and social responsibility. Many "test"-related issues are being related to equal opportunity issues and policies.

VI. CONCLUSION

Four major sections were discussed in the chapter—The Promise of *Brown*, Significant Court Cases, Social Forces and Civil Rights, and Educational Inequality. These sections serve to highlight politics contained in the concept of equal educational opportunity.

The Promise of *Brown* discussed the hopes and aspirations for the *Brown* decision along with the intent of the decision. Significant Court Cases were discussed to serve as a background for the Department of Education's current equal education policies. Social Forces and Civil Rights addressed the events leading to the enactment of the Civil Rights Act of 1964, which served as the rationale for the Department of Health, Education, and Welfare's need to set a national policy on equal education matters. Educational Inequality was discussed to give evidence of issues over time which are related to access to education and outcomes. These issues effect equal opportunity and educational policy.

The factors identified set the stage for discussing the Department of Education's school desegregation enforcement effort. These historical factors led to the Department's current inconsistent application of educational policy. As stated previously, these factors reveal competition among interest groups and individuals for equal educational policy initiatives. Politics has played this significant role in the government's inconsistent enforcement of educational policy. Figure 1 provides a timeline of major events from 1954 to 1981.

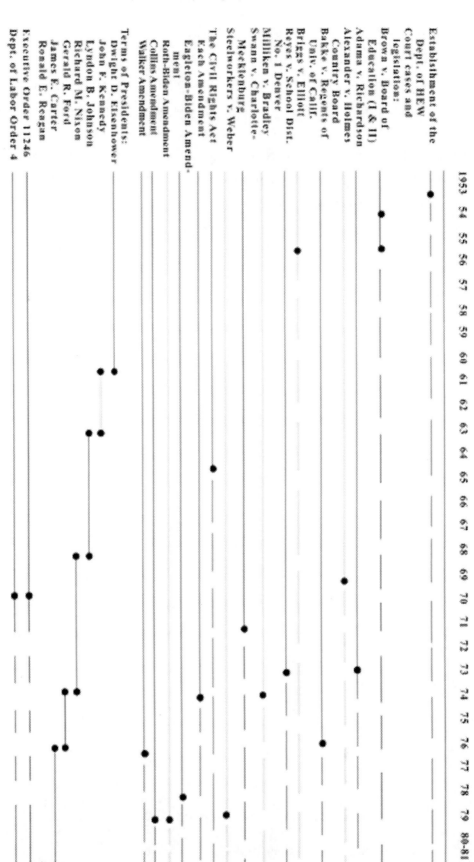

Figure 1. - Timeline of Major Events from 1954 - 1981

CHAPTER II

THE FEDERAL GOVERNMENT ENFORCEMENT EFFORT AND THE *ADAMS* LITIGATION

This chapter will identify the Department of Education's school desegregation enforcement effort and identify reasons why the agency has been inconsistent in its enforcement of equal education policy. Additionally, the reasons for the *Adams* litigation will be thoroughly discussed.

The major argument is that the Department of Education has been derelict in its duties to enforce applicable provisions of the Civil Rights Act of 1964, as well as its own policies formulated to address this law. Additional information reviews and documents the Department of Education's policies which relate to school desegregation. The discussion of the *Adams* litigation focuses the declaratory judgment and the injunctive order the U.S. District Court decreed in the case *Adams v. Richardson*. The injunctive order mandates the Department of Education to enforce Title VI of the Civil Rights Act as intended by Congress.

In view of efforts to implement equal educational opportunity, the executive branch's practices and policies are discussed. This information highlights the thesis by providing evidence of the lack of enforcement in the HEW's Office for Civil Rights. The case *Adams v. Richardson, 480 F 2d 1159 (1973)* illustrates the failure of HEW's Office for Civil Rights to carry out its statutory responsibilities when school systems are in violation of court orders to desegregate.

Many messages from the White House direct agency chiefs to perform certain duties. An administration's philosophy on certain matters—in particular, school desegregation—an agency chief may enforce compliance with desegregation laws depending upon the President who happens to be in office. Therefore, policies can change based on an administration's philosophy.

Due to different presidential office holders during the period 1953 to 1981, the compliance philosophy in school desegregation matters changed dramatically. Under the Nixon administration, the philosophy adopted was one of "benign neglect." The Nixon administration's posture was to permit the Justice Department to play an active role in enforcing compliance through litigation instead of requiring HEW's Office for Civil Rights to initiate Federal fund cut-off efforts. Under the Carter administration, the HEW (OCR) took a more active role in enforcing compliance due to the specific orders given in the *Adams* litigation. Therefore, during the period there are different enforcement philosophies. Presidential power and politics have played a role in the Department of Education's compliance effort. The political maneuvering by the "President's men," which include the executives in the various agencies and departments, has effected the Department of Education's compliance effort.

The Chief Executive, the President of the U.S., is the chief administrative officer of the Federal Government. Under the executive branch of government fall the "executive" agencies. The Constitution of the United States grants the President "Executive Powers." He/she is charged to see that the laws are "faithfully executed," which suggests a general administrative responsibility; but duty is not power. He/she also enjoys express powers, such as the power to make appointments. Still other authority is conferred by acts of Congress and by weight of custom (Koenig, 1968, p. 155).

Congress's influence is its unique control over agency bureaucrats through special committees and subcommittees.

> By tradition Congress is closely involved in personnel administration. In detailed laws, Congress sets down the elements of a classification structure, rates of pay, service ratings, retirement, and the like. (Koenig, 1968, p. 157)

The above statements highlight the Congressional role of personnel administration. The "Executive" relies on key staff members to administer the Federal Government bureaucracy. The Chief Executive's staff, again, utilizes its influence and special concerns to oversee key domestic issues.

The President's constituencies also play a vital role in his re-election, and as a public leader he attempts to provide direction for the nation. The Chief Executive's relationship with Congress, his constituencies, and public opinion effect his leadership capabilities.

> One leadership role that the President plays is that of "conservator." In this role the President is viewed as guardian of the existing order, of social, economic, and political parts. He maintains programs and policies initiated by his predecessors or at most extends them, but in a fashion consistent with hallowed patterns of the past. He reverses precedent and established procedure. (Koenig, 1968, p. 184)

The "conservator" leadership role of the President maintains precedent and preserves established procedure.

After reviewing the above theme, one can determine the various types of roles the President displays in the leadership process. Certainly, there are checks and balances on his power; however, significant managerial authority comes with the Executive Office of the President.

> The United States Supreme Court, which in ruling on civil rights and Congressional districting thus befriended Presidential power, may well come in some future day to strengthen his power as administrative chief. The necessary judicial ingredients are at hand in the sweeping "executive power" clause. (Koenig, 1968, p. 189)

The "executive power" clause is vague, and the President's future power may be determined by future events.

There are different ways to conceptualize Presidential power:

> One way is to focus on the tactics, so to speak, of influencing certain men in given situations: how to get a bill through Congress, how to settle strikes, how to quiet Cabinet feuds, or how to stop a Suez. The other way is to step back from tactics on those "givens" and to deal with influences in more strategic terms: what is its nature and what are its sources?

The above statement highlights two ways power can be conceptualized. The focus will address influence in strategic terms. The latter approach will be the approach given to the study of the Department of Education. As society becomes more complex, different problems will effect presidential leadership. Upon reviewing Presidential power, it is important to look at the leadership styles of different officeholders. When studying equal opportunity in education, the policy focus will become different with each President. The Federal Government enforcement effort in equal educational opportunity varied differently with each administration. The various approaches to equal opportunity in education reveal the lack of access protected class members received under the Civil Rights Act of 1964. Again, politics played an important role in Presidential leadership.

In 1961 when the Congress was considering major legislation that proposed Federal aid to education, President "Kennedy made clear that he was adamantly opposed to any Federal aid to schools, the parochial schools. The Constitution clearly prohibits aid to the schools, to parochial schools" (Paper, 1975, p. 273). Later, in another state, President Kennedy adopted a different position on the same issue.

For when his public statement of opposition ignited a vigorous outspoken response by the Catholic church and its supporters in Congress, Kennedy made a tactical retreat: at a press conference a week later he said that Congress could debate the question of special purpose loans to parochial schools; his earlier remarks, he observed, had concerned only across-the-board grants to elementary and secondary schools. (Paper, 1975, p. 274)

The above statements reveal the shift in President Kennedy's position on the same issue. This political shift in position is not unusual and is involved in political decision making.

I. THE CIVIL RIGHTS ACT OF 1964

After the Civil Rights Act was passed in 1964, Title VI of the Civil Rights Act was the administrative tool used for the enforcement of nondiscrimination in education. The Department of Education now enforces these provisions through its Office for Civil Rights.

In 1969, however, the use of administrative enforcement procedures under Title VI was sharply curtailed and persuasion largely replaced sanctions. After 1971, there was a further curtailment in desegregation suits by the Government. This change produced delays in desegregation and a lack of results in which the Supreme Court soon expressed its impatience. (U.S. Comm. on Civil Rights, 1975, p. 46)

These statements reveal the decreased enforcement of the Act since its passage and Supreme Court reaction to delays in desegregation..

The Civil Rights Act of 1964 has two major components:

(a) It prohibits discrimination on the basis of race, color, religion, or national origin.

(b) It prohibits discrimination on the basis of race, color, religion, sex, or national origin by employers, unions, and employment agencies. In addition, it beefs up the protections afforded minority groups in voting, in using public facilities, in attending public schools, and in seeking employment on projects involving Federal funds. The two titles of the Act which had important implications for education were Title IV and Title VI.

Title IV – Public Schools. Although desegregation in public schools was officially outlawed by the Supreme Court in 1954, the Civil Rights Act gave the U.S. Attorney General the authority to bring lawsuits against school boards and public colleges. Prior to filing a lawsuit, a complaint must be in writing and a school board or college must be given ample time to adjust its practices. The alternate emphasis of the title is to give the U.S. Office of Education assistance in the process of desegregation.

Desegregation is defined as the

assignment of students to public schools without regard to race, color, religion, or national origin, but not to mean assignment of students to schools to overcome racial imbalance—programs, that is, of the type where students may be taken by bus to school miles from their homes—to maintain a racial "mix" comparable to that of the community as a whole. (Civil Rights Act of 1964, P.L. 88-352, 7-2-1964)

The statement clearly defines desegregation as stated in the Civil Rights Act and used in this study.

Other aspects were also contained in the Act which authorized that controversial survey—the Coleman Report. The technical assistance provisions of the Act operated to provide assistance to public schools planning for school integration. The Commissioner of the Office of Education had no enforcement responsibility.

Title VI. Title VI relates solely to Federally assisted programs. It reads:

No person in the United States shall, on the ground of race, color, or national origin, be excluded from participation in, be denied the benefits of, or be subjected to discrimination under any program or activitiy receiving federal financial assistance. (Civil Rights Act of 1964, P.L. 88-352) 2

The first sentence sets the tone for the title, although it is broad in scope. It also extends to Federal Government agencies a statement, accompanied by rules and regulations banning discrimination. Again, the Department of Education now enforces these provisions of the act.

During the fall of 1973, the Office for Civil Rights (OCR) conducted a survey and found that there were 16,698 public school systems serving 45,499,000 students (DHEW, 1973). The funding these school districts received totaled billions of dollars allocated under the jurisdiction of Title VI of the Civil Rights Act of 1964. Currently ED's Office for Civil Rights (OCR) is responsible for monitoring Federally funded public elementary and secondary school districts and non-public schools benefiting from Federal programs and ensuring compliance with civil rights provisions. Responsibility under Title VI includes overseeing the elimination of all vestiges of unlawful segregation and enforcing the requirements of the May 25, 1970, memorandum issued to school districts by OCR, which specifically defines districts' responsibilities to overcome discrimination against national origin minority group children (Memorandum from J. Stanley Pottinger, May 25, 1970). The U.S. Office of Education worked with OCR in selecting and reviewing school districts under the Emergency School Aid Act (ESAA). ESAA funds are used to assist in school desegregation. The OCR has responsibility for ensuring civil rights compliance under ESAA and the court injunction in *Adams v. Richardson* (480 F.2d 1159 [D.C. Cir. 1973]).

II. POLICIES ON ELEMENTARY, SECONDARY SCHOOL COMPLIANCE WITH TITLE VI

HEW's compliance policies are specific where applicable to the elimination of dual systems in voluntary segregation plans. Generally, all school systems within the scope of the title are required to eliminate all dual systems and establish unitary systems. Compliance with the law requires integration of students, black and white, faculties, facilities, and all activities. In situations where voluntary compliance has not proved successful, a desegregation plan designed to ensure compliance must be developed and implemented. There are a variety of ways in which a school system can ensure compliance, and students' assignments can occur in a number of ways. The OCR recommends various methods to eliminate dual systems which are designed to provide methods which expeditiously comply with the Act. The following methods are not organized in any particular way. The methods are the full range of options outlined by the OCR.

Freedom of Choice Plans. Freedom of choice plans generally require students and their parents to choose a school of their choice (free choice). However, when these plans are not effective, other methods are necessary to achieve compliance. In numerous instances, additional methods needed to bring about the desired results.

Geographic Attendance Zones. To eliminate dual school systems, school districts must, when applicable, rearrange geographic attendance zones. The significant factor in eliminating the dual structure. HEW's guidelines require that:

School systems are responsible for assuring that to the extent it is administratively feasible, the zone boundaries do not perpetuate any vestiges of a dual school structure and that among the various attendance zone arrangements which are possible, it establishes the one which best promotes elimination of its dual structure. (DHEW, 1964, p. 8)

This statement reveals HEW policy on the rearrangement of geographic attendance zones.

Reorganization of the School Structure. Under the dual system, school structures must be reorganized to eliminate separate systems. Examples of how this can be accomplished are: a middle school concept that provides classes for students in grades 7 and 8. Grades 9 through 12 can be taught in a high school. Any reorganization designed to restructure a school system and provide equal opportunity to the students will be acceptable under this provision as long as the other provisions as stated in Title IV are complied with.

School Closings. School closings are often used to eliminate dual systems. Generally school closings are used with a combination of methods. One problem that may develop is the failure to integrate the faculty in the schools that are currently open (Sec. 601, 602, Civil Rights Act of 1964; 78 Stat. 252; 42, U.S.C. 2000d, 200d-1).

School Construction and Consolidation. Consolidation of existing schools or new schools is often necessary to eliminate dual school systems. A school's faculty can also be affected unless it is integrated into the existing schools during these consolidation efforts. When the construction of new schools is necessary, site selection is important. The school site must be neutral to provide equal access for all pupils.

New and Special Educational Programs. The provision applies to any and all new educational programs including special educational programs. These programs must be integrated to eliminate the recurrence of a dual school system. Programs such as adult education, special education, summer school, etc., are covered under this provision.

Transportation (Busing). Transportation systems must be reorganized to eliminate dual bus routes. The transportation system must provide for the assignment of students to buses without consideration of race, color, or national origin (Sec. 601, 602, Civil Rights Act of 1967; 78 Stat. 252; 42 U.S.C. 2000d, 200d-1).

Attendance Outside the System of Residence. The provision prohibits school attendance outside the pupil's system of residence and makes illegal any arrangement which provides attendance outside the system of residence.

The previous discussion describes the policy provisions that HEW (OCR) maintains regarding schools eliminating dual systems pursuant to a voluntary desegregation plan. The following policy provisions relate to the entire compliance program. Policies regarding school eliminating dual systems are different than policies regarding the entire compliance programs. The elimination of a dual system is an element of the entire compliance program.

Voluntary Compliance. The OCR also suggests school officials voluntarily comply with Title VI of the Civil Rights Act to eliminate discrimination based on race, color, or national origin. Voluntary compliance is written into the law; and prior to any penalty authorized by the HEW, the voluntary compliance provision provides the first step in the process.

Advice and Assistance. The OCR provides advice and assistance to school districts undergoing voluntary or non-voluntary compliance. The national office and the regional offices provide any assistance necessary in achieving compliance with the law (Sec. 602 Civil Rights Act of 1964; 78 Stat. 252; 42 U.S.C. 2000d-1).

Technical Assistance. This type of aid is provided by the U.S. Office of Education under Title VI of the Civil Rights Act. Technical assistance in the form of preparation and implementation of desegregation plans is provided. Under special circumstances where school districts are undergoing problems associated with desegregation, university centers provide assistance. These programs are funded under Title IV of the Act (Sec. 602, Civil Rights Act of 1962, 78 Stat. 247; 42 U.S.C. 2000d-1).

Reports and Reviews. The department requires reports and conducts compliance reviews with school systems deemed in non-compliance. These periodic reports determine assurance of compliance. The OCR staff conducts on-site reviews to monitor compliance.

Negotiations Concerning Non-compliance. When school systems are found in non-compliance, negotiations are conducted to point out areas of non-compliance and to suggest methods which ensure compliance. The school system is given a written explanation of the problem and upon request voluntary assistance is provided for problem resolution. Negotiations that lead to agreement are committed to writing with specific directions. The negotiation process is determined by reports and reviews, and it is the last step in the compliance procedure prior to enforcement action (Sec. 602, Civil Rights Act of 1964, 78 Stat. 242; 42 U.S.C. 2000d-1).

Cooperation with State Education Agencies. HEW requires school systems to cooperate with state education agencies. These agencies are apprised of school systems which are in violation of Title VI.

Enforcement Action. HEW applies enforcement action whenever school systems fail to assure compliance. The agency's enforcement action takes two forms:

1. Administrative proceedings designed to terminate Federal financial assistance funds
2. Referral to the Justice Department for appropriate legal action

Prior to a termination order, administrative hearings are held before hearing examiners. Termination orders are then referred to Congressional committees which have oversight responsibility (Secs. 603, 604, Civil Rights Act of 1964; 78 Stat. 252, 253; 42 U.S.C. 2000d-1, 2000d-2).

III. AFFIRMATIVE ACTION POLICY INTERPRETATION

The following discussion highlights policies unique to affirmative action. These policies are different from those in the previous analysis. In the Affirmative Action Policy (AAP) Interpretation dated October 10, 1979, HEW emphasized the voluntary affirmative action plan of admitting minority students to institutions of higher education. The policy is specific to criteria which would be utilized while developing the AAP. The objectives of the policy are consistent with the decision in *University of California Regents v. Bakke* (438 U.S. 265, 1978 [*Bakke*]). The policy cannot set aside a fixed number of positions (quotas) for minority students for which they cannot compete. The policy under Title VI of the Civil Rights Act precludes institutions of higher education from remedying discrimination by employing voluntary affirmative action. These steps to affirmative action are designed to overcome the present effects of past discrimination. Much controversy has centered around this issue in discrimination cases. The opponents considered affirmative action synonymous with "preferential treatment." Much latitude is given to educational institutions which develop Affirmative Action Plans. Institutions considering voluntary affirmative action can develop additional and alternative techniques for inclusion in voluntary plans. HEW's affirmative action policy guidelines under Section 803(b)(6) Civil Rights Act of 1964 45 C.F.R., addresses institutions which have previously discriminated against persons. Remedies cited include affirmative action as a means of overcoming the effects of past discrimination.

In these cases, the institution must make its programs equally available to all persons regardless of race, color, and national origin. The institution's efforts along these lines must show active recruitment practices designed to promote the availability of theinstitutional programs. Finally, these policies are applicable to both public and private educational institutions which receive or benefit from Federal financial assistance under HEW's jurisdiction. The policy also applies to students who participate in HEW-funded or guaranteed student loan assistance programs (*Federal Register*, October 10, 1979).

Case-related Memoranda. From time to time HEW's Office of Standards, Policy, and Research (OSPR) published a digest of significant case-related memoranda. The OSPR attempts to ensure that compliance determinations are consistent with established policy. Generally, these policy issues arise during investigations and compliance reviews conducted by HEW staff. The memoranda address issues under Title IX of the education amendments of 1972, Title VI of the Civil Rights Act of 1964 and Section 504 of the Rehabilitation Act of 1973.

One example of case-related memoranda issued by the Office of Standards, Policy, and Research involves the issue of discrimination on the basis of race, color, or national origin in employment where the purpose of the Federal financial assistance is to provide employment. For example:

OCR received a complaint filed by a handicapped, minority employee of a state rehabilitation agency whose employment was terminated on May 12, 1977. During his employment the complainant was also a client of the agency. The Federal financial assistance to the state rehabilitation agency was designed to assist handicapped persons obtain gainful employment.

The OCR gave the following decision:

> Under Title VI, employment jurisdiction exists where a primary objective of the Federal financial assistance is to provide employment. Since a primary objective of the assistance was to provide employment, OCR has employment jurisdiction under Title VI.
>
> It is a Departmental policy to investigate complaints filed prior to the effective date of the Department's 504 regulation, June 3, 1977, only if the complaint charges a violation of the statute that does not require the interpretive language of the regulation for resolution. Thus, the Department will investigate a case alleging employment discrimination on the basis of handicap before June 3, 1977, only if adjustments would not have been needed to accommodate the applicant's handicap. In this case the incident complained of occurred before June 3, 1977, and the issue is adjustment to accommodate the complainant's handicap. As a result, the action complained of is not considered unlawful. (Office for Civil Rights, June and July 1979)

The objective of federal financial assistance is to provide employment. OCR cited the policy decision based on its Title VI regulation and Section 504 of Policy Interpretation No. 1. These case-related memoranda are published from time to time for clarification of agency policy and guidelines as they relate to the agency's Title VI responsibility under the law.

The following factors will explain the Department of Education's lack of uniformity in enforcing school desegregation policy. The lack of uniformity relates to the Civil Rights Act and the Department's own policies in that the Civil Rights Act set the broad policies in terms of law, and the Department's own policies set out compliance provisions.

IV. THE *ADAMS* LITIGATION

In *Adams v. Richardson*, the plaintiffs alleged that HEW violated the Civil Rights Act of 1964 and the fifth and fourteenth amendments by failing to terminate Federal funds to elementary and secondary schools, colleges, and universities which continued to practice unlawful discrimination. At the time of the *Adams v. Richardson* order, J. Stanley Pottinger, Director, OCR, affirmed that compliance with the injunction would increase by 40 percent the normal workload of the OCR staff during the first 90 days of implementation (U.S. Comm. on Civil Rights, 1974, p. 14). This statement by Pottinger was very ambitious; however, OCR's problems were more comprehensive than just staffing patterns. The problem areas that existed in 1974 included:

a. Development of guidelines on requirements
b. Requirements that states assume responsibility for securing voluntary compliance
c. Requirements for self-analysis and affirmative action
d. Implementation of administrative sanctions

OCR's current situation cannot be appreciated without an understanding of the *Adams* litigation. Rulings and orders from this litigation control and planning and scheduling of much of the enforcement work and supporting activities for all three of the major civil rights laws.

During the late 1960s, OCR's primary activity was the dismantling of racially dual school systems in the south. These efforts were effective. Hundreds of southern school districts were desegregated. Administrative proceedings were initiated against hundreds of school districts, and funds for many were terminated.

At the same time, OCR began examining school districts in the north. Also, they began investigations in ten southern states to determine whether the states had desegregated their former racially dual systems of higher education. After initial investigations, North Carolina, Virginia, Georgia, Florida, Arkansas, Oklahoma, Maryland, Pennsylvania, Mississippi, and Louisiana were advised that their systems had not been desegregated fully.

In the early 1970s, the NAACP Legal Defense and Education Fund (LDF) filed suit against HEW in the United States District Court for the District of Columbia. The case, then styled *Adams v. Richardson*, alleged that the Department was failing to enforce Title VI in both elementary and secondary education and higher education in the 17 southern and border states. Plaintiffs sought orders requiring the Department to process complaints within specified time frames, to complete compliance reviews in progress, and to begin others.

In 1973, U.S. District Judge John Pratt ruled for the plaintiffs. He held that HEW was failing to fulfill its responsibilities under Title VI. During the next few years, Judge Pratt issued a series of orders requiring action on specific cases and ultimately imposing procedural requirements and time frames on the processing of all complaints and compliance reviews. Judge Pratt issued specific requirements regarding the completion of the agency's higher education desegregation activities. The orders also required the Department to review every southern school system that had racially identifiable schools.

A unique feature in *Adams* is the agency's defense to the lawsuit. The agency claimed the administrative "discretion" exception to the general rule that agency action is reviewable under the Administrative Procedures Act. The Court construed this exception narrowly and stated that the exception is only applicable in situations where the statutes are drawn in broad terms where there is no law to apply. The Court ruled that Title VI of the Civil Rights Act was specific in its terms and there was no reason for the agency to claim administrative discretion. In addition, the Court found the OCR had "consciously and expressly adopted a general policy which was in effect an abdication of its statutory duty," and consistent failure to do so is reviewable in the courts as dereliction of duty.

The decision in *Adams* gave consideration to the OCR for its inexperience in desegregation problems related to colleges and universities. Despite the fact that the HEW-OCR was inexperienced in desegregation problems in colleges and universities, guidelines were formulated for desegregating statewide systems of higher learning. These guidelines did not comment on desegregation plans submitted and did not justify the department's failure to comply with the Congressional mandate. Again, the Court allowed the exception for inexperience; however, that issue is entirely different from enforcing compliance. The District Court prior to appeal gave the agency the following order:

> The District Court found appellants' performance to fall below that required of them under Title VI, and ordered them to (1) institute compliance procedures against ten state-operated systems of higher education, (2) commence enforcement proceedings against seventy-four secondary and primary school districts found either to have reneged on previously approved desegregation plans or to be otherwise out of compliance with Title VI, (3) commence enforcement proceedings against forty-two districts previously deemed by HEW to be in presumptive violation of the Supreme Court's ruling in *Swann v. Charlotte-Mecklenburg Board of Education, 402 U.S. 1, 91 S.Ct. 1267, 28 L.Ed.2d 554 (1971)*, (4) demand of eight-five other secondary and primary districts an explanation of racial disproportion in apparent violation of *Swann*, (5) implement

an enforcement program to secure Title VI compliance with respect to vocational and special schools, (6) monitor all school districts under court desegregation orders to the extent that HEW resources permit, and (7) make periodic reports to appellees on their activities in each of the above areas.

We modify the injunction concerning higher education and affirm the remainder of the order. (Adams v. Richardson, 480 F.2d 1159 [1973] 1161)

The statements detail the elements of the injunctive order set down in *Adams*.

On appeal, the agency reasserted its argument by maintaining that the agency has absolute discretion and that it attempts to achieve voluntary compliance in most instances. The Appeals Court found this argument untenable in light of the specific wording in the statute. The following statements highlight the Court's review of the agency defense to the lawsuit.

Each Federal department and agency which is empowered to extend Federal financial assistance to any program or activity... is authorized and directed to effectuate the provisions of section 2000d of this title with respect to such program or activity by issuing rules, regulations, or orders of general applicability.... Compliance with any requirement adopted pursuant to this section may be effected (1) by the termination of or refusal to grant or to continue assistance under such program or activity to any recipient as to whom there has been an express finding on the record, after opportunity for hearing, of a failure to comply with such requirement... or (2) by any other means authorized by Law: *Provided, however,* That no such action shall be taken until the department or agency concerned has advised the appropriate person or persons of the failure to comply with the requirement and has determined that compliance cannot be secured by voluntary means.... (42 U.S.C. §2000d-1)

The defense of absolute discretion is untenable in light of the foregoing statements. However, the aspect of the defense to the lawsuit which deals with the lack of personnel appears plausible and creditable. The Appeals Court in *Adams* did highlight and take account of the unique role of the traditionally black college and university, which states:

The problem of integrating higher education must be dealt with on a statewide rather than a school-by-school basis.[10] Perhaps the most serious problem in this area is the lack of statewide planning to provide more and better trained minority group doctors, lawyers, engineers and other professionals. A predicate for minority access to quality post-graduate programs is a viable, coordinated stateside higher education policy that takes into account the special problems of minority students and of Black colleges. As *amicus* points out, these Black institutions currently fulfill a crucial need and will continue to play *an important* role in Black higher education.[11]

[10]It is important to note that we are not here discussing discriminatory admissions policies of individual institutions. to the extent that such practices are discovered, immediate corrective action is required, but we do no understand HEW to dispute that point. This controversy concerns the more complex problem of system-wide racial imbalance.

[11]The brief is that filed by the National Association for Equal Opportunity in Higher Education, a voluntary association of the presidents of 110 predominantly Negro colleges and universities, both state-supported and private. (Adams v. Richardson, 480 F.2d 1159 [1973] p. 1165)

The unique role the appeals court attributed to traditionally black colleges and universities was plausible and creditable.

Additionally, the District Court affirmed that HEW has a monitoring function when school districts are under Court order to desegregate. Upon realizing that the Court which determined the order also had the responsibility for its enforcement, the injunction specified that HEW had responsibility to assist in the monitoring of such orders.

On Wednesday, February 15, 1978, HEW published in the *Federal Register* "Revised Criteria Specifying the Ingredients of Acceptable Plans to Desegregate State Systems of Public Higher Education." In 1969 and 1970, HEW's OCR notified ten state school systems of their failure to remedy and to dismantle statewide dual systems of segregated education. The states were Arkansas, Florida, Georgia, Pennsylvania, and Virginia. Under the *Adams v. Richardson* decision, HEW directed six states to "submit within 60 days of receipt of criteria a revised desegregation plan within 120 days thereafter" (*Federal Register*, February 15, 1978). The states responded to HEW's request. However, after negotiation, HEW only accepted the desegregation plans of Arkansas, Florida, and Oklahoma. The plans of Georgia, North Carolina, Mississippi, Maryland, and Virginia were not accepted. The revised criteria addressed a statewide approach of eliminating unlawful dual systems as opposed to a school-by-school approach. The criteria addressed admissions, recruitment, retention, placement and distribution of faculty, and duplication of program offerings, and the enhancement of the role of traditionally black colleges. This discussion highlights the ingredients for monitoring state systems of public higher education.

It was determined that HEW had the responsibility to monitor school systems' court orders to desegregate.

The enhancement of the role of traditionally Black colleges was included in the revised criteria for desegregation plans in higher education. Heretofore, HEW's enforcement effort was seriously lax in higher education. Again, in the *Adams* case, the Court emphasized:

> Perhaps the most serious problem in this area is the lack of state-wide planning to provide more and better trained minority group doctors, lawyers, engineers and other professionals. A predicate for minority access to quality post-graduate programs is viable, co-ordinated state-wide higher education policy that takes into account the special problems of minority students and of Black colleges. These Black institutions currently fulfill a crucial need and will continue to play an important role in Black higher education. (Adams v. Richardson, 408 F.2d at 1164-1165)

In a supplement District Court Order in 1977, the Court of Appeals, stated,

> The process of desegregation must not place a greater burden on Black institutions or Black students' opportunity to receive a quality public higher education. The desegregation process should take into account the unequal status of the Black colleges and the real danger that desegregation will diminish higher education opportunities for Blacks. Without suggesting the answer to this complex problem it is the responsibility of HEW to devise criteria for higher education desegregation plans which will take into account the unique importance of Black colleges and at the same time comply with the Congressional mandate. (*Federal Register*, February 15, 1978)

These statements mean that HEW has oversight responsibility for Black colleges under Title VI. However, when discriminatory systems of higher education need dismantling, the state must take care in fashioning a remedy designed to reaffirm the role of traditionally Black colleges and to eliminate the unconstitutional dual system. The criteria are general, and the elements of the plan are as follows. First comes the disestablishment of the structure of the dual system. Second, each desegregation plan shall:

a. Define the mission of each institution within the state system on a basis other than race and the mission statement shall include:

1. The level, range and scope of programs and degrees offered;
2. Geographic area served by the institution; and
3. The projected size of the study body and staff, for each year of the life of the plan.
b. Specify steps to be taken to strengthen the role of the traditionally black institutions in the state system. (*Federal Register*, February 15, 1978)

Other components of the revised criteria for acceptable state desegregation plans contain the desegregation of student enrollment, the desegregation of faculty, administrative staffs, nonacademic personnel, and governing boards, and the submission of plans and monitoring. Other lawsuits alleging similar *Adams* violations have been filed.

In 1975, the NAACP Legal Defense Fund (LDF) filed a second suit against HEW, alleging precisely the same failures with respect to elementary and secondary education in the 33 northern and western states. This case was *Brown v. Weinberger*. It was assigned to Judge Sirica, who in 1976 also ruled for the plaintiffs and held that HEW had failed to fulfill its responsibilities in the north as well. He, too imposed time frames on the processing of complaints and the completion of compliance reviews.

Additionally, in 1974, the Women's Equity Action League (WEAL) filed a suit similar to *Adams* and *Brown* alleging that the Department was failing to enforce Title IX of the Education Amendments of 1972. This case was never resolved on the merits, but was settled in December 1977.

Current Status of Adams, Brown, and WEAL. In early 1977, OCR was faced with two problems regarding the *Adams, Brown,* and *WEAL* litigation. First, Judge Pratt had held that the plans the Department had accepted from North Carolina, Virginia, Georgia, Florida, Arkansas, and Oklahoma were unacceptable.

The second problem was that the agency was not complying with the procedural orders in *Adams* and *Brown* regarding the processing of complaints. The complaint backlog was growing steadily. Very few complaints were processed in a timely fashion, and many compliance reviews remained unfinished.

As a consequence, plaintiffs in both *Adams* and *Brown* were prepared to return to court to seek additional relief. At the same time, plaintiffs in *WEAL* were pressing their claim for relief against the agency. With respect to the latter, the agency's poor record regarding enforcement of Title IX revealed there was no credible defense.

The Department was successful in settling all three cases in a consent order in December 1977. The basic provision of the order requires that HEW use its best efforts to eliminate the complaint backlog by the end of FY 1979-September 30 1979. This extended period of time for the elimination of the backlog was negotiated because the department wanted to reserve some staff for the completion of existing compliance reviews and the initiation of new ones. The order also established slightly revised time frames for the completion of complaint investigations and compliance reviews after September 30, 1979.

The settlement was made possible because the Office of Management and Budget (OMB) agreed to seek from Congress an additional 898 positions requested in the OCR budget proposal for FY 1978. This was important to the plaintiffs because one allegation was that the previous administration had failed to seek sufficient staff to handle the complaint workload, and the department failed to fill authorized positions approved by the Congress.

In 1978 the positions were approved by Congress. Due to improved management, OCR planned to be in compliance with the *Adams* order by the end of fiscal year 1979, as required. To date the OCR is not in compliance with *Adams*.

Adams stated specific guidelines:

> The injunction does not direct the termination of any funds, nor can any funds be terminated prior to a determination of noncompliance. In this suit against the agency, in contrast to actions brought against individual school systems, our purpose, and the purpose of the District Court order as we understand it, is not to resolve particular questions of compliance or noncompliance. It is, rather, to assure that the agency properly construers its statutory obligations and that the policies it adopts and implements are consistent with those duties and not a negation of them. With this broad purpose in mind, we turn to the substance of the order. We have examined the record in relation to the findings of fact made by the District Court, and can only conclude that they are unassailable. (Adams v. Richardson, 480 F.2d 1159 [1973] 1163)

These statements highlight the guidelines in *Adams* which attempt to assure the agency properly construes its statutory obligations and policies..

The *Adams* plaintiffs alleged three material predicates of their motion for a summary judgment. These three areas are 1) failure to investigate, (2) refusal to commence enforcement proceedings, and (3) abandonment of the suspension-termination authority.

Failure to investigate

Generally, the plaintiffs stated that the HEW had failed to assert its authority to school districts under desegregation orders. In the case the cause of action rested with the Fountain

Amendment (42 U.S.C. 2000d-5). The amendment exempts HEW from those Title VI functions only with school districts "in compliance with... a final desegregation order or federal court judgment." At the time of the case the HEW had failed to exercise any jurisdiction in court-order districts (Adams v. Richardson, Pottinger affidavit of December 7, 1970, p. 3, 2210) and that even though " no actual legal barrier prevents" HEW from doing so (Holmes affidavit of March 24, 1971, p. 4), it did not monitor court-order districts to determine whether they were in fact in compliance. The HEW's position asserted that the Fountain amendment is satisfied when school districts merely provide assurance that they will comply. Actually, HEW's refusal to investigate school districts under desegregation decrees was not following the provisions of the Fountain amendment. More important, not only had HEW abstained from investigating court-order districts, but special schools and vocational schools administered by state departments of education were neglected.

In the hearings, HEW admitted it would expand its enforcement efforts to state vocational educational agencies and initiate compliance reviews. The statements in the hearing served as an admission of the agency's failure to fulfill its investigatory responsibility. A unique aspect of HEW's defense is that the department did not deny, explain, or attempt to defend its total failure since 1964 to exercise its Title VI jurisdiction over numerous vocational and special schools (for the deaf, blind, etc.) administered by the state. Clearly, in refusing even to investigate whether school districts under desegregation decrees are complying with their court orders, HEW, in effect, rewrote the Fountain amendment to excise its "compliance" qualification. It appeared HEW had concluded that the Fountain amendment, predicated on "compliance" with a desegregation decree, is satisfied when a school district subject to a final order just states it will comply. The plaintiffs in the case were concerned that HEW provide more than an admission of neglect of duty, but provide some attempt to show future compliance. The agency attempted to do that, but failed.

Refusal to initiate enforce-
ment proceedings

From the affidavits in the case, Director Pottinger, and Acting Director Holmes, did not deny that more than two years ago (from the time of litigation) HEW found ten states to be operating racially segregated higher education systems. To date, the agency did not exercise its enforcement proceedings. HEW's submissions in the case also failed to identify specific steps to secure compliance from school systems. At thetime of the litigation, HEW had not submitted an outline for assuring compliance from ten states that were found in violation of Title VI. Much of the defiance of the department stemmed from the department's failure to commence enforcement proceedings in higher education. More importantly, HEW's failure to enforce compliance in the years 1968-69 and 1969-70 in school districts which had reneged on their HEW-approved desegregation plans further penetrated the "administrative discretion" defense. In 1970, Mr. Pottinger's (former director, OCR) affidavit contained a statement that 81 new renege cases had been found. IN fact, HEW had not at the time of the litigation commenced enforcement action against any school district in the 12-month period while Mr. Pottinger was director. Although "renege" cases were pending action in the regional office, at the headquarters level in the agency's Office of the General Counsel, the cases had received no action, the ten previous "renege" cases were referred to the Justice Department.

Aid termination and suspension

HEW ceased final terminations of funds in non-complying school districts. In 1968, HEW issued fund terminations to 46 segregated school districts as opposed to 1969 where HEW issued fund terminations in only four districts. Moreover, since the period 1968-1981, no school districts had fund terminations. HEW currently maintains the first essential step in the final termination process is a notice beginning formal enforcement proceedings. To date, HEW had not invoked any fund termination proceedings against non-complying school districts.

Beyond the stop in fund-terminations, HEW had ceased resort to aid suspension or "deferral" power. HEW's past policy was to defer only funds for "new" programs which continued to make payments to violators of Title VI on previously approved "continuing" school aid plans. The plaintiffs in the case asserted that HEW would not suspend school aid programs of violators while having knowledge of the 81 school districts that reneged on HEW-approved desegregation plans, the Department failed to defer or suspend grants-in-aid to districts, and HEW also had no evidence of "voluntary compliance" on behalf of school systems. HEW's liability through the years was an unduly restrictive aid suspension policy which permitted some school districts to defy the agency with impunity. This action on the desegregation plans submitted to HEW was negligent.

In *Alexander v. Holmes*, the Supreme Court ruled that since HEW had failed to move against the 87 districts whose September desegregation plans became constitutionally inadequate on October 29, 1969, the court's ruling to districts was to "desegregate at once." In the *Alexander* case, HEW refused to terminate or defer funds from districts which refused to comply. The various 87 school districts which were undeniably in violation of Title VI simply continued to receive Federal aid for the remainder of the school year notwithstanding their failure to update their desegregation plan timetables. In point of fact, another flagrant violation of HEW's dereliction of duty is obvious in the Osceola, Arkansas, school district, where HEW granted the school district an additional year to desegregate. In Stanley Pottinger's affidavit, he stated that HEW was in error and that the Osceola case was referred to the Justice Department for litigation in February 1972. More than a year after *Alexander*, Osceola was being permitted to continue to receive Federal funds in violation of the Constitution and Title VI. One course of action HEW could have followed would have been to suspend or place Osceola's Federal funds in escrow. It is suspected that this course of action would have brought the school district into immediate compliance.

In essence, the above information shows the total default of HEW's compliance effort in the area of investigation, compliance proceedings, and aid suspension-termination. This information also highlights the Senate Select Subcommittee on Equal Educational Opportunity's finding of HEW's neglect of enforcement of hundreds of school districts in 1972. HEW's response in the subcommittee was its "admittance" to varying degrees of noncompliance in 87 districts and others. HEW officials did assert that when it fails to secure voluntary compliance from renege districts it takes expeditious action to refer the cases to the Department of Justice for litigation.

On July 3, 1969, Attorney General John Mitchell and Secretary Finch of HEW announced a new policy to "minimize the number of cases where it is necessary to employ the fund cut-off remedy. This policy was due to HEW's numerous fund cut-offs which were effected in 1967 and 1968 along with HEW's former use of the aid suspension power. Currently, many of these means of enforcement have ceased. Actually, since the end of the 1969-1970 school year, HEW's enforcement record was simply non-existent. As stated in the plaintiffs' memorandum in support of their notice of deposition,

> Futile and ineffective exhortation of violators to mend their ways has replaced any and all enforcement methods; essentially Title VI had become a dead letter in the area of segregated public schooling.

This statement describes HEW's lack of policy enforcement.

HEW's functions under Title VI
of the Civil Rights Act of 1964
regarding Public Higher Education

As noted earlier, HEW in 1969 found the state of Louisiana was operating a racially segregated system of higher education. HEW also made a similar determination with respect to the state systems of higher education in Mississippi, Oklahoma, North Carolina, Florida, Arkansas, Pennsylvania, Georgia, Maryland, and Virginia. In letters to the ten states, HEW requested each of them to submit a desegregation plan within 120 days or less. Some of the states—Louisiana, Mississippi, Oklahoma, North Carolina, and Florida—totally ignored HEW's requests and never submitted a desegregation plan. However, Arkansas, Pennsylvania, Georgia, Maryland, and Virginia submitted to HEW a desegregation plan which was found unacceptable. HEW filed formally to comment on any of these submissions in the intervening years.

However, HEW did not begin enforcement action against any of the states nor had the Justice Department received any of the cases for litigation. HEW's practice of advancing funds to the states had continued despite the unacceptabiligy of the states' desegregation plans. HEW's defense in *Adams* relates to the agency's posture of negotiation with the school systems. HEW also maintained that these negotiations were complex and that the Supreme Court's standard in *Alexander* "to desegregate at once" did not apply to higher education systems. HEW's compliance with Title VI has been negligent. To delay enforcement proceedings against the affected states is against the provisions of the 1964 Civil Rights Act. The agency's continuation of financial assistance to public school systems violated the letter and spirit of the law. Having determined that a state system of higher education was in violation of Title VI and failed to achieve voluntary compliance, the protected class members under the act had their rights violated.

Again, in the "Declaratory Judgment and Injunction Order" in the *Adams* case (February 16, 1978), United States District Judge John H. Pratt enjoined HEW to begin enforcement proceedings to effect compliance with Title VI by the states of Louisiana, Mississippi, Oklahoma, North Carolina, Florida, Arkansas, Pennsylvania, Georgia, Maryland, and Virginia. In addition, the agency had to report all steps taken to comply with the injunction, including a description of the Justice Department's actions in any public higher education's violations. The agency also had the responsibility to report to the court every six months for three years to permit the court's evaluation of delays by the agency in light of enforcement procedures.

Additionally, the agency was ordered to describe each complaint of racial segregation or discrimination in public higher education received by the agency. Also within 120 days of receipt of such complaint or other information, the agency had to provide an explanation for reason and determination whenever enforcement proceedings have not been commenced within 90 days of an HEW finding of racial segregation or discrimination.

HEW's functions under Title VI
of the Civil Rights Act of 1964
concerning renege or noncompli-
ance districts

During 1970-73, 113 elementary and secondary school districts were found by HEW to have reneged on prior approved desegregation plans or to be otherwise out of compliance. Out of the 113 districts referred to the Justice Department, only three districts were sued by the department. Albeit HEW's knowledge of 98 school districts in noncompliance since early 1970-71, 74 school districts at that time were out of compliance, and no enforcement proceedings were initiated by the agency. The 74 districts had also continued to receive Federal financial assistance from HEW. As usual, HEW's defense was its negotiation and conciliation procedures with districts to assure voluntary compliance.

The injunction in the *Adams* case (1973) required and enjoined the agency to begin enforcement proceedings by administrative notice of hearing or to utilize any other means authorized by law to effect compliance with Title VI. The agency was also required to report all steps taken to comply with the injunctive order, including a description of what action the Justice Department had taken in cases referred to the agency. After a six-month period and for three years after the order, the department had to present to the court any reasons for delays by the agency in bringing enforcement proceedings. To effect this, the department was ordered to do the following:

(a) Give a description of each complaint or other information of racial segregation in public elementary and secondary schools.

(b) Whenever within 90 days of receipt of a complaint, and no administrative determination was made by the agency, an explanation of the specific reasons for failure to make a determination had to be given to the court.

(c) Any determination based on a complaint where a finding of presence or absence of segregation or discrimination, a specific reason had to be given.

(d) Last, whenever enforcement proceedings had not begun within 60 days of a finding of segregation or discrimination, a reason for failure to commence enforcement must be given. (Adams v. Richardson, Declaratory Judgment and Injunctive Order, February 16, 1973)

In light of the *Alexander v. Holmes County Board of Education, 396 U.S. 19 (1969)*, the Supreme Court required desegregation "at once" of all dual systems. At the time of the decision (October 29, 1969) HEW-OCR had approved desegregation plans in 87 school districts which permitted desegregation to be postponed until September 1970. In objection to the ruling in *Alexander*, the agency took no steps to enforce compliance against the 87 school districts in the year 1969-1970.

Also with the Supreme Court ruling in *Swann v. Charlotte-Mecklenburg Board of Education, 402 U.S. 1 (1971)*, which stated a "presumption against schools that are substantially disproportionate in their racial composition." At that time, HEW identified 300 non-court order school districts where at least one or more of the 300 school districts were composed of local minority students. Initially, HEW eliminated 75 of the 300 districts from further consideration without any on-site investigation or communication. The rationale HEW gave to the court was that the disproportionate number was too small to consider in light of *Swann*. Then HEW eliminated 134 of the remaining 225 without any investigation or on-site investigation. Additionally, none of the remaining districts were required to give justification for the substantial racial disproportion in the school districts. HEW mailed letters to the remaining 91 school districts notifying them of additional steps that may be required under the *Swann* decision. In response to the department's notification, 37 school districts sent desegregation plans to HEW that were acceptable. In 42 cases, the school districts were deemed in presumptive violation of *Swann*; and at the time of the lawsuit, a year after the findings, HEW had not taken any additional enforcement action.

In 85 of the school districts with one or more schools substantially disproportionate in racial composition, HEW continued to give financial assistance to the school district in violation of Title VI of the Civil Rights Act. HEW's responsibility is to require school districts in violation of *Swann* to explain or rebut their practices. Additionally, in 1971 HEW found 42 of the school districts in presumptive violation of *Swann*. In 1973, when the declaratory judgment was rendered, HEW had not begun enforcement proceedings.

In the injunctive order, the agency was given 60 days to communicate with each of the 85 school districts listed in the judgment and put them on notice to explain or rebut the substantial racial disproportion in one or more of the district's schools. Also, the order required HEW to begin enforcement proceedings by administrative notice of hearing or to use any other means prescribed by law to ensure compliance. Prior to the court's November 16, 1972, memorandum opinion, HEW did not make a determination of compliance.

The order in *Adams* required HEW to give an account of the action taken in cases referred to the Justice Department in addition to the other requirements. Also every twelfth month after the issuance of the order for a three-year period, a list of all school districts in the

17 southern states whose percentage of local minority pupils in the last academic year were 20 percent disproportionate from the local minority pupils in the entire district had to be explained or rebutted to the agency.

HEW's functions under Title VI
of the Civil Rights Act of 1964
concerning vocational and other
schools administered by state
departments of education

The Declaratory Judgment also referred to schools operated by states for the deaf, blind, and mentally handicapped children. In the 17 southern and border states, HEW gave information that a total of 205 schools operated for such purposes. HEW did not supply specific data that related to race; however, it did supply data which revealed that Louisiana had obvious racial segregation, whereas seven of such state administered schools were black and 25 were overwhelmingly white. Prior to the *Adams* litigation, there was no such enforcement effort related to these types of schools. After the lawsuit, a program was announced, but never initiated, to enforce state schools administered for the deaf, blind, and mentally handicapped. HEW's announced effort only related to vocational schools in the south. HEW continued to distribute federal funds. Thus, in this instance, the agency was in violation for continuing to administer Federal financial assistance. The attorneys in the case argued that the agency violated the plaintiff's rights protected by the Act and that the rights of those "similarly situated" were also violated. In the injunction, the agency was required to implement without delay an enforcement program adequate to ensure compliance with Title VI with respect to vocational schools and schools administered or operated by state education departments. The attorneys for the plaintiffs were successful in the injunction in having the agency submit the following data (*Adams v. Richardson*):

1. All schools administered or operated by state departments of education where HEW has found reason to believe or suspect that racial discrimination or segregation may be practiced

2. The date of each on-site investigation by HEW compliance officers at each of the schools listed in the preceding paragraph, or the reasons for HEW's failure to make such investigation

3. The steps taken by HEW to secure compliance by such schools with Title VI and the Constitution

These requests were mandated within 150 days of the order and every twelfth month after the order was issued.

*HEW's functions under Title VI
of the Civil Rights Act of 1964
concerning school districts
subject to court desegregation orders*

Of the 640 school districts which received HEW aid, all of the school districts were subject to school desegregation court orders in the 17 states. In the declaratory judgment, it was pointed out that after the signing of the 1964 Civil Rights Act, HEW deemed a district in compliance if it were subject to a final desegregation order and provide assurance of compliance. In the 1968 amendments to the 1964 Civil Rights Act, HEW reaffirmed its position; for HEW's purposes, an educational agency was in compliance with Title VI when the agency was in compliance with a final court desegregation order. Once a school district had been placed under a court desegregation order and given assurance "on paper" that it was in compliance with the order, HEW routinely accepted it as fact. The agency did not monitor the school districts to determine whether or not they were in compliance. The agency defended its position by asserting (a) its lack of resources, (b) its conflicts with the courts, and (c) its possible conflicts with the Justice Department. HEW's continued advancement of Federal funds to school districts under court order further complicates matters.

Compliance by school districts and other educational agencies under a final order of a Federal court for the desegregation of the school or school system operated by such agencies, is by virtue of 42 U.S.C. §20000d-5 to be deemed compliance with the provisions of Title VI. Until there has been a finding by the court entering the order that its order has not been complied with, defendants are under no obligation to effectuate the provisions of Title VI through administrative or judicial enforcement proceedings. (Adams v. Richardson)

HEW's negligence was in the area of monitoring school districts under court order and bringing school districts in non-compliance to the attention of the courts. The agency was enjoined to monitor all school districts under court desegregation orders. The agency was also required to provide in verified form data listing all districts subject to court desegregation orders, along with findings of each court order violation.

When HEW initiates administrative enforcement proceedings, its practice was to defer the school districts application for "new" programs funds only. HEW never made any attempt to recapture funds distributed to a district between the notice of hearing and a final determination of Title VI ineligibility. HEW's defense is that the statute has no provisions for recapture of funds. Since the agency's administrative enforcement proceedings generally continue over a number of years, HEW's limited deferral practice allows the continued flow of Federal funds to school districts.

Last, after HEW had initiated enforcement proceedings and action to terminate federal funds, the agency had no authority to withhold federal funds on previously approved plans. Prior to termination of funds, the agency must make a report to the Congress sand then only terminate funds after a 30-day period. The injunction enjoined HEW to provide verified data to the attorneys for Adams el al. every six months after the order. Specifically, the agency had to provide a list of each notice of hearing issued to a public education institution, along with a list of the termination action and a listing of each report of the head of the agency to the Congress. The report also had to state the basis for the action precluded by Title VI of the Act and the amount of funds paid by the agency after initiation and during pendency of enforcement proceedings until termination actions become effective.

As late as July 14, 1981, the plaintiffs in the continuing case now titled *Adams v. Bell, Civil No. 70-3095* filed a supplemental memorandum in support of a hearing request. In the supplemental order dated April 1, 1977, Judge Pratt ordered the ED-OCR to find compliance or non-compliance within 90 days of the commencement of a compliance review or acknowledgment that a complaint has been received. As late as June 17, 1981, Secretary Bell and the OCR disregarded the directive of the court by placing a hold on 80 to 100 draft letters of findings (LOF's) which propose to find a violation of the Civil Rights Laws. This practice is uniquely different from Secretary Hufstedler's (his predecessor), who cleared proposed LOF's for release within seven days on the average (Adams v. Bell, 70-3095, filed July 14, 1981). On July 14, 1981, 86 cases were "on h old" in the Secretary's office, including six which are 174 days old and 34 which are from 117 to 145 days old. This action is paramount to placing the cases in an indefinite "limbo," which has come long after processing and investigation.

As the ED-OCR continually defies court orders ensuring compliance, the *Adams* litigation, which began in 1971, continued in 1981 to seek remedies for plaintiffs asserting their civil rights under the law. It appears the agency's default was not unintentional. In the plaintiffs' points and authorities in support of motion for summary judgment, the attorneys for the plaintiffs stated:

Instead of compliance, months and years after receiving HEW notification that they were violating Title VI by racial practices school districts and higher education systems continue discriminating in violation of the Constitution, of *Alexander*, and Title VI. HEW's default is not an oversight, but rather reflects a deliberate policy to abstain from use of the paramount duty under Title VI. Only this court's intervention can restore the spirit and the letter of Title VI in the area of public education.

These statements reflect HEW's deliberate policy to abstain enforcing equal education policy in violation of Title VI of the Civil Rights Act of 1964. It also appears the default was not unintentional.

CHAPTER III

THE ADMINISTRATIVE FUNCTION OF THE
DEPARTMENT OF EDUCATION

This chapter argues that there are various administrative factors which explain reasons for failure to enforce the law. Prior to identifying the department's administrative function in school desegregation policy (e.g., coordination, complaint processing system), I will discuss the administration of regulatory statutes and the concept of "discretionary justice." A discussion of the administration of regulatory statutes highlights the department's defense to the *Adams* litigation. The department's defense was again "administrative discretion." An appreciation of the administrative function is important to understand the complex nature in which the ED carries out its administrative activities. ED's inefficiency in this area is due in part to the discretion given the administrative function and the interpretation of that function as perceived by policy makers in the department. An explanation of the administrative function is necessary to show that educational policy has been inconsistently enforced at the national level.

The plaintiffs in the *Adams* case perceived the agency as being derelict in its duty to administer and enforce the law in the public interest. After discussion of the issue with ED personnel active with the agency during the period, one Equal Opportunity specialist stated: "The agency had problems responding to the Congress and political winds of the times; therefore, there was no consistent Federal voice on the administration of these matters" (A. Besner, Department of Education, Office of Civil Rights, October 23, 1980). Additionally, there are also problems with coordination (e.g., administration) within the department. Before discussing the specific problems with the agency, a discussion of organizational complexity and regulation must follow.

The documented problems which follow in this chapter again reveal the problems of complexity in organizations. A case in point is Anderson and Warkow's study of "Organizational Size and Functional Complexity" (1961). The authors found:

> One of the important problems in any organization is the coordination
> of the various activities which occur within it. This coordination function is
> normally performed by the administrative component of the organization. The

relative size of this component is an important dependent variable in much organizational theory. In particular, the coordination of activities is alleged to become relatively more difficult (requiring a more than proportionately greater expenditure of time or energy or both) with an increased number of personnel and with a greater variety of role activities or tasks. (p. 23)

The statements describe the importance of the coordination function in organizations and their relative size. One of the reasons for reorganization of HEW in 1979 was due to its size. The new U.S. Department of Education was established at that time. At the time of reorganization and the establishment of the Department of Education (ED), HEW was the largest Federal agency.

This treatment of the administrative function and its relationship to educational policy enforcement describes some of the problems of regulation. Complaint processing during the period was plagued with large backlogs of cases, which is another aspect of the administrative process. A feature presented is that one of the ideals of regulation is the broad construction of statutes. Broad construction is a principle whereby a statute is given a liberal interpretation. In the last chapter, HEW's defense was its administrative discretion in enforcement, and the court applied the narrow, specific interpretation. The past events reveal that HEW gave the statute a liberal interpretation; however, the court found the agency used its discretion in the wrong way.

This discussion applies to situations where the legislation has directed reforms of existing practices to protect groups and societal interests regardless of whether the formal basis of the regulation is (a) a statutory requirement prohibiting certain conduct, or (b) a statute or other law (e.g., Executive Order) which determines conditions as related to the receipt of Federal grants and contracts, licensure, when the agency performs its duty regulating a practice or function. Again, the need for broad discretion and consistency suggests developmental aspects of the administrative process.

I. THE ADMINISTRATION OF REGULATORY STATUTES

Since 1964, the Department of Health, Education, and Welfare (HEW), now Department of Education (ED), has administered compliance with Title IV and Title VI of the Civil Rights Act of 1964. Many groups have criticized the ways these statutes have been administered. Failure of modern reform legislation has been attributed to the ineffective administration of new regulatory statues (Blumrosen, 1977, pp. 87-114, 209-237).

The administrative process is a means to implement substantive law. If a regulatory statute is to have significant impact, it must be broadly construed at the outset, because the operation of the legal system will ultimately "water down" or narrow its thrust. An agency may adopt and apply the principle of broad construction. But experience has demonstrated that too much is asked of administrators if they are allowed to adopt or reject construction principles at their discretion. The rule of discretion leaves the administrator exposed to and unprotected against various pressures with neutralize the agency. (Blumrosen, 1977, p. 88)

Blumrosen highlights the legal principle of broad construction of statutes as important in administration. This writer also adopts that view.

Given the fact that the Congress enacts legislation and does not clearly define the prohibited practices, the administrative agency has broad discretion to administer statutes. It is left to the agency to determine the extent of the definition and the extent of compliance necessary to meet the Congressional mandate. Many researchers believe the administrative process may be responsible for the ineffective administration of regulatory statutes (Comptroller General, 1976 [HRD 76-142]).

II. DISCRETIONARY JUSTICE

Legal scholars have studied administrative law and developed the concept of "discretionary justice" (David, 1969, vi-vii). Davis suggests the desirability of restricting, organizing, and limiting discretion within existing policies and not issues of broad policy. The focus on discretion relates to the molding of policy by administrators and the methods used to implement such policies to understand the wide ranges of policy alternatives.

Blumrosen (1977) suggests that:

The failure of administrators to make full and effective use of their processes is itself an exercise of their discretion. This failure is less accessible to study and evaluation than are concrete actions in individual cases. It is only when the range of choices open to administrators has been observed and understood that it becomes feasible to develop standards to determine if the administrator has performed adequately in making these choices. Thus the many empirical studies of administration in action provide a matrix within which the administrator's judgments can be evaluated. (pp. 87-114)

Blumrosen highlights the failure of administrators to make full and effective use of their discretion to understand the wide range of policy alternatives.

Based on the activities stemming from the "Watergate" scandal, many have argued for limiting administrative discretion. In a Congressional report titled the "Moss Report," the staff of the House Subcommittee on Oversight and Investigations studied the regulatory practices of nine Federal agencies. The report addressed the quality and efficiency of Federal regulation. Therefore, in the aftermath of the "Watergate" scandal, Congress's emphasis has been to maintain quality and efficiency in its regulatory function. Given these problems, agency administrators cannot turn to Congress for any sagacious guidance or answers to their problems. Many scholars have attempted to address this problem. Rosenblum (1972) and Robinson (1970) believe it is important to plan research into strategies for administration. However, Blumrosen (1977, p. 29)

maintains that when administrative strategies are developed, two problems arise:

a) the understanding of each regulatory situation in terms of the technology involved and the history and policy of the particular statute

b) political consideration affects the entire implementation process—appointing the agency personnel, budgeting, influencing particular decisions

Blumrosen suggests it is important for strategic planning in administration.

Administrative policies and practices can be analyzed from one agency to another. Many of the shortcomings (in terms of administrative process) of one agency are similar to the problems in another. In the case of the ED (OCR) and the Equal Employment Opportunity Commission (EEOC), the interpretation of both titles under the Civil Rights Act generally has the same effect—that is, to remedy discrimination in America's institutions. Blumrosen (1977) disagrees with those who advocate that a general legal analysis cannot be applied to regulatory agencies. In terms of political considerations, legal analysis does not negate a general theory of administrative process. Blumrosen's general theory could assist in the ED meeting fully its Congressional mandate. Blumrosen's general theory discusses "the ineffectiveness of the administrative process" in executing reform legislation and proposes that administrators be required "to adhere to the principle that reform legislation is to be broadly construed" (p. 87).

III. CIVIL RIGHTS ADMINISTRATION

The Equal Employment Opportunity's Commission's administrative practices can be compared to ED's practices. Each agency has administrative responsibilities under the Civil Rights Act of 1964.

In employment discrimination, the Equal Employment Opportunity Commission (EEOC) has received public criticism for the ineffective administration of Title VII of the Civil Rights Act of 1964. The EEOC in the early years developed significant case law which gave the agency a strong "posture" on interpreting the Civil Rights Act. However, other problems developed. The agency was plagued with a growing backlog of charges (complaint processing system) which prevented it from effectively discharging its responsibilities under the law. Charging parties who filed complaints of discrimination waited many months before receiving a determination. It took 24 months to resolve a complaint from the date it was initially filed.

In 1977 President Carter appointed Eleanor Holmes Norton as the new chair of the EEOC. Ms. Norton previously held the chief executive position with the Human Resources Administration of New York City Commission. In August 1977 at the Senate confirmation hearing, Mrs. Norton responded to an inquiry alleging that the government spoke with "a forked tongue" and emphasized the Congressional mandate in relationship to the administrative process. Therefore, the administrative process is, and can be, critical to the effectiveness of regulatory statutes. Supreme Court Justice Frankfurter stated,

> Administration is more than a means of regulation. Administration is regulation. We have been concerned with a complex and interrelated federal scheme of law, remedy and administration. (San Diego Building Trade Council et al. v. Carmon et al., 359 U.S. 236, 243 [1959])

Justice Frankfurter's statements reveal the administrative process is critical to the effectiveness of regulation.

Bureaucrats often interpret legislation by focusing on Congressional intent. EEOC was involved in the civil rights case *Griggs v. Duke Power Co., 401 U.S. 424, 91 S.Ct. 849 (1971)*. EEOC construed Title VII of the Civil Rights Act broadly. The Supreme Court upheld EEOC's administrative decision finding that "disparate effect" in employment was discriminatory. This discussion of disparate effect theory gives some idea of the broad interpretation of the EEOC used in addressing its administrative function. The disparate effect theory in employment cases occurs when an employer uses a criterion or decision-making practice which is seemingly unbiased, but which actually serves to exclude a disproportionate number of persons on a prohibited basis. When examining neutral criteria and decision-making processes for possible discrimination, one can utilize the disparate effect theory.

The implementation of this theory involves the use of criteria which seem unbiased and uniformly applied. First, it is necessary to identify the criteria used and then to ensure that these criteria apply to all individuals equally. A criterion is a standard against which people are judged to determine if they are eligible for hiring, promotion, etc. Criteria are considered neutral if they appear to treat all individuals the same regardless of race, color, national origin, or religion. Neutral criteria generally fall into three categories: physical characteristics, test performance, and personal background. Background criteria generally relate to an individual's accomplishment or experience, such as education, work history, arrest records, awards, community service, participation in extracurricular activities.

The broad construction the EEOC accorded the regulatory statute assisted in the development of its current effective administration.

Prior to the *Griggs* decision, two other theories of discrimination were operable: (1) the intentional theory of discrimination or the "evil motive" theory, and (2) the unequal treatment theory. It is apparent that it would be hard to measure or determine the motivation of a discriminator. The unequal treatment theory or disparate treatment theory focused on the discriminatee as his situation/condition related to others similarly situated. The rationale underlying *Griggs* provided for a "systemic" perception of discrimination, which gave the administrative agency broad statutory construction powers.

To give some example of the assessment of the ED-OCR administrative function, in 1974 the U.S. Commission on Civil Rights published an across-the-board evaluation of Federal civil rights enforcement (*The Federal Civil Rights Enforcement Effort, 1974*, vol. 3: *To Ensure Equal Educational Opportunity*, p. 384). . After scrutinizing OCR's efforts, the following recommendations were offered:

1) OCR should improve its data collection system. In this area, OCR's efforts were lax. Its information systems failed to reveal data on faculty, ethnic group composition, or dropout rates.

2) OCR should promptly issue comprehensive guidelines delineating the equal education opportunity responsibilities of public schools. The Commission felt that HEW's guidelines did not cover adequately student transportation, disciplinary action, and metropolitan school

desegregation concerns. Furthermore, an analysis of school systems was called for to assess the distribution of personnel and services. In 1974, the guidelines looked to affirmative action provisions for systems not in compliance with the act. HEW's guidelines failed to address specific procedures for conducting compliance reviews.

3) OCR should take steps to ensure that its compliance reviews of school districts dealt effectively with the range of possible non-compliance. This recommendation suggested that HEW consider the full range of non-compliance—specifically, the existence of racial isolation in urban areas with added consideration given to interdistrict violations of the law. This provision would address metropolitan forms of discrimination which had been inadequately considered in HEW's previous guidelines. The voluntary compliance feature of the agency's policies should also address negotiated settlements and include specific remedies that related to goals, objectives, and timetables.

4) "Although it is recognized that OCR compliance reviews are more sophisticated than in prior years and that it has begun to review large city districts, the extent of its reviews must be stepped up" (*The Federal Civil Rights Enforcement Effort*, 1974, Vol. III: *To Ensure Equal Educational Opportunity*, p. 384).

5) OCR practices should assess compliance of state education agencies. This recommendation addressed state education policies with respect to discrimination. To ensure their compliance, the state role in eliminating racial isolation in the public schools should be examined to determine exacerbation of non-compliance or the decrease in the isolation. The accountability of state agencies in securing compliance of school districts must also be reviewed. This recommendation is important in light of the fact that there is much local power and control in local school districts. Spring (1978) contends:

> Increasingly, the major governing roles of local boards and school administrative staffs are as interpreters and administrators of educational policies dictated at the state and federal levels. This is still an important function, because the board and administrative staffs can influence the execution of a segregation order from the courts or the federal Office of Education. In some communities desegregation has been accomplished with a great deal of success because of the cooperation of the school board; in other communities the exact opposite has occurred.

Again, Spring's analysis depicts the influence state education agencies may have in exercising the compliance function.

6) OCR should increase its efforts to ensure that non-public schools which receive direct or indirect Federal assistance do not discriminate on the basis of race, national origin, or sex.

It is suggested that HEW adopt guidelines for non-public schools. Additionally, compliance reviews of these systems should be initiated. Historically, HEW activity in this area has been lax. It is also suggested that HEW coordinate its activities with the Internal Revenue Service and coordinate joint compliance reviews and share information. Many critics have asserted that Federal regulatory agencies may have more effective administration given coordinated Federal activity. Some agencies have overlapping jurisdiction which can effectively ensure compliance given coordinated activity.

7) OCR should investigate and resolve all complaints it receives in a timely fashion. This recommendation is appropriate in light of the *Adams v. Richardson* litigation. HEW failed to adequately discharge this responsibility in the past and present. The complaint resolution rate is extremely low. Again, this problem in HEW is quite similar to EEOC's past charge resolution and remedy problems. As this chapter indicates, the general problems in regulatory agencies related to the administrative function.

8) In cases involving probable non-compliance when OCR's negotiations with the recipient do not result within 90 days in an adequate written agreement in which the recipient is to take corrective action pursuant to a fixed timetable, OCR should immediately initiate sanction proceedings. Proceedings should be warranted in all cases where school systems are in non-compliance and have not requested an extension. It is further recommended that these extensions are not to exceed 30 days. In the forthcoming chapter, "The Congress and School Desegregation," Congressional actions which have limited HEW-OCR's ability to fulfill its mandate are discussed. Although all of Congress's actions were not finalized, it would be interesting to determine the effect of these actions upon HEW's top management officials. As legislation is introduced, agency officials may misinterpret the appropriate administrative response. It is recommended that the school districts involved in the *Adams v. Richardson* case be brought into compliance within 90 days or be subjected to administrative sanction proceedings for Federal financial assistance termination.

9) After determining how implementation of the above recommendations would increase its capacity for enforcing the law, OCR should request the additional staff needed to fulfill its compliance responsibilities (*The Federal Civil Rights Enforcement Effort*, 1974, Vol. III: *To Ensure Equal Educational Opportunity*, pp. 381-386). Staff shortages have always been a problem at OCR. In addition to its staffing problems, OCR's administrative function and administrative process present limitations. A general theory of administration which gives broad construction to the regulatory statute is needed. The recommendations by the U.S. Commission on Civil Rights offered OCR's administration plans which were designed to increase compliance with the appropriate titles of the Civil Rights Act. The regulatory agency has a responsibility to enforce the law as set down by the Congress. Often problems arise that relate to interpretations of the

statutes; therefore, it may be that the regulatory agency is "not in step" with the Congress. As stated earlier, generally the bureaucrat attempts to interpret the statutes in terms of the "intent" of Congress. To date, the OCR has not fulfilled the Civil Rights interpretation of the law at the time of its enactment.

IV. COMPLAINT PROCESSING

ED-OCR fails to satisfy its complaint processing requirements in the administration of Title VI. ED-OCR accepts complaints from individuals and groups. ED-OCR also addresses complaints from school districts. However, those complaints from individuals and groups (NAACP, CORE) that pertain to possible discrimination violations are not given proper attention or consideration. The fact that a citizen or civil rights group has filed a complaint alleging specific problems is not enough to initiate an OCR investigation and a determination.

In Fiscal 1973, the OCR's Education Division received a total of 498 complaints, according to the complaint logs of ten regional offices. Of that number 177 (35 percent) came from northern and western states. The complaints ranged widely, from one objecting to the use of an Indian as a mascot at a high school in Pocatello, Idaho, to a charge of racial discrimination in the discharge of a teacher in Dayton, Ohio. Of the 177 complaints, another 12 percent were resolved by a finding of insufficient evidence of discrimination. A few of the cases took a long time to be resolved... one took nine months, another 17. (Sometimes records were not clear either as to the date of the complaint or of its resolution.) (Center for National Policy Review, 1974, p. 65)

This information indicates complain processing by ED-OCR was viewed as a nuisance rather than as an aid to remedying discrimination. It is also a fact that OCR uses a minimum of staff time and effort to investigate and resolve such complaints. OCR's staff had a habit of questioning the complainants' charges and motivation for bringing the charges. As investigations are carried out, all elements of a complaint are not addressed. OCR glosses over allegations that have been investigated with bureaucratic language. Rather than give the complainant full information about his case, the complainant generally receives the same response from OCR that the school districts give to the OCR.

There are numerous administrative approaches which, if implemented, could remedy some of OCR's complaint processing problems. At OCR, complaint processing functions administratively as a "process service" rather than regulatorily. OCR is charged with the responsibility of enforcing civil rights statutes. When responding to complaints, OCR generally contacts institutions via the mail. Occasionally "on-site" investigations are conducted; but such investigations may not produce the information necessary to resolve a complaint adequately. In other words, discrimination is not eliminated "root" and "branch." When responding to a complainant, OCR often fails to contact the parties and apprise them of different aspects which arise (Center for National Policy Review, 1974, pp. 65-70).

Administratively, OCR fails to enforce civil rights statutes adequately; and when court action is pending, OCR often suspends enforcement action. OCR also suspends enforcement action while conducting negotiations with school districts which are litigants or defendants. Once one understands that many of these court cases are administratively tied up, one gains an awareness into the length of time spent making such determinations. In the public's eye, ED is perceived as a vehicle which serves the public, without court action. When court action is initiated, the failure of ED to act in the public's behalf flies in the face of the letter and spirit of the law in the *Brown* case and the Civil Rights Act of 1964.

> For example, the Westwood, Michigan, school district case of OCR was suspended in 1972 when the district was included as one of several dozen districts in a possible metropolitan desegregation plan for the city of Detroit. The Detroit school case, filed in 1970, was not decided by the Supreme Court until July 25, 1974. Meanwhile in Westwood, Michigan, faculty hiring and assignment discrimination, *de jure* pupil segregation in three of the seven schools, and unequal educational services at these schools remained uncorrected, despite the fact that these probable Title VI violations were documented by OCR investigators nearly three years ago. (Center for National Policy Review, 1974, pp. 67-70)

The above example highlights the length of time OCR takes in making determinations. The preceding case indicates that OCR would not violate any of its statutory regulations by enforcing the law and requiring a school district violator to comply with the statute.

OCR also suspends enforcement when the Department of Justice is involved. OCR often requests that the Department of Justice become involved prior to final determination.

> However one assesses the record of the Justice Department in handling
> school desegregation cases, it does not appear that HEW's practice of voluntarily

relinquishing jurisdiction can be justified on grounds that referral to Justice is a means to speedy and effective relief for result is to permit federal aid to continue for years to districts in probable violation of Title VI, notwithstanding HEW's primary duty to see that discrimination is ended in programs which it funds. (Center for National Policy Review, 1974, p. 71)

These statements highlight HEW's practice of relinquishing jurisdiction to the Justice Department.

The second major criticism of HEW-OCR is HEW's failure to act on evidence of discrimination. After the investigation team visits a school district, often areas of compliance not previously addressed require further investigation. This kind of investigation requires repeated trips to the school district. This method of investigation displeases school officials and raises doubts as to the purpose of the investigation. Officials may also interpret repeated visits as harassment. To understand the necessity for repeated trips to school districts, we must first understand the complex jurisdictional issues involved. Generally, ED/OCR investigates three areas of compliance: discrimination in selection and assignment of faculty, discrimination in desegregation plans and pupil assignment, and discrimination in vocational programs. When faced with uncharted or controversial jurisdictional problems, OCR may need to repeat visits; but generally such a practice antagonizes the school system.

The reporting of findings is also a problem, since OCR's reports are often disjointed and emphasize minor facts or practices and not major violations of the law. OCR reports generally follow a departmental compliance format, which is spelled out in a document entitled "Basic Components of a 441 Review." For example, in a Utica, New York, case an OCR report emphasized minute details without relating these details to the significant areas of non-compliance which the agency was supposed to investigate. Th e allegations in the Utica case were as follows:

1) racially imbalanced schools
2) discriminatory recruitment, assignment, and promotion of black teachers
3) over-representation of minority children in educable mentally regarded (EMR) classes

The case became so muddled it was referred for litigation through HEW's Office of the General Counsel (OGC). The OGC and OCR are partly repsonsible for HEW's failure to act on evidence obtained in its field reports. Before initiating litigation, OGC will request that OCR forward voluminous information on cases to its department. OGC's rationale is that such information is necessary to prove discrimination based on evidentiary grounds. Once OCR has gathered the requested evidence, OGC will turn around and request that OCR gather additional data, because OCR's original findings of evidence were inconclusive or "stale."

In a Dayton (Ohio) case (*Dayton v. Brinkman, 45. U.S.L.W. 4910, 4913-4914*, June 27, 1977), OCR spent approximately four months gathering data supporting a finding of non-compliance and turned it over to the OGC. OGC, in turn, requested additional data from OCR. The Dayton case addressed the following issues: faculty assignments, inferior facilities, inadequate facilities, and pupil assignment. The pupil assignment issue was difficult to prove from the existing evidence. Therefore, OGC returned the file to the OCR.

The Dayton public school system had a total of 34 percent black enrollment. Of the 69 schools, 20 schools had more than 95 percent black enrollment, and 22 schools had more than 95 percent white enrollment. OCR documents showed that Dayton had maintained a "dual system" since 1915. Additional areas of non-compliance were Dayton's segregated faculty, discriminatory school site selection, and utilization of discriminatory attendance zones. Before bringing litigation, the OGC maintained it needed supporting data on each school from 1915 to the present to substantiate a charge of *de jure* segregation. OGC also requested automatic data processing equipment to assist in the investigation (Memorandum to J. Stanley Pottinger from Roderick Potter of the Civil Rights Division, OGC, 1977).

During the processing stage, so many data were needed to prove the allegations filed against the Dayton school system that the private parties involved refused to negotiate, thereby tying up the case in bureaucratic red tape. Finally, the NAACP filed a lawsuit which brought the Dayton school system into court and suspended HEW's non-compliance processing procedure.

The Dayton case is just another example of a harmful administrative process. The victims of discrimination do not have their grievances resolved in an efficient, timely manner. Furthermore, this type of administrative process fails to address the letter and spirit of Title VI of the Civil Rights Law by inadequately enforcing the law in the public's interest. ED's complaint processing system is plagued with lax enforcement efforts. OCR and OGC had staffing shortages which were being ignored. Although OCR has had its staff increased, OGC has not (to any significant degree) and work overloads were prevalent.

Many of the problems which have a negative effect on the ED enforcement effort stem from the agency's administrative function. This administrative function can be viewed from two distinct perspectives: (1) the management practices need revision and coordination, (2) coordination of offices within the agency would assist in alleviating many of the practices discussed previously—specifically, the problems between the OCR and the OGC. Again, the EEOC's transformation is a good example (Center for National Policy Review, 1974).

During the 1977 Reorganization of the Federal Civil Rights effort under the Civil Service Reform Act, the EEOC, a principal agency in the initiative, redesigned, redirected, and reoriented its personnel to comply with the administration thrust (EEOC: The Transformation of an Agency, 1978).

Under President Carter's Reorganization Plan No. 1, the Congress approved the plan to reorganize the Federal Government's equal employment enforcement activities. The plan consolidates equal employment opportunity programs and sets the stage for a coherent Federal voice. The reorganization play of the agency emphasized investigative teams and attorneys to work on cases simultaneously. The purpose of this effort was designed to assist attorneys in obtaining "litigation worthy data" to be used in court and also to assist investigators in obtaining subpoenas and other devices necessary to compel compliance. From the start, this activity coordinates the investigation staff with the legal staff, and the effective enforcement of the statute can be obtained.

Again, the broad interpretation of the statute should be used to assist in effective administration.

The principle of broad construction of social legislation has a long and honorable history. But administrations have not been required to follow the principle, even though the modern administrative apparatus was established to achieve reforms which are promoted by the principle of liberal construction. The principle emerged out of the struggle to accommodate judge-made law with the mass of legislation enactments. (*Harvard Law Review*, 1980)

Early judicial hostility to legislative reforms was reflected by the maxim requiring narrow construction of statutes in derogation of the common law. This gave way in time to the thrust of legislative reform which was not blunted by judicial hostility. (National Labor Relations Board v. Hearst Publications, 322 U.S. 111 [1941])

The above statements support the use of the broad interpretationa of the statute.

Finally, to achieve effective administration of regulatory statutes, broad construction of the law and management capability are necessary for effective compliance. It is necessary that further research investigate methods designed to achieve effective administration and bolster the administrative function of the agency.

The concept of "discretionary justice," if applied to ED's policy thrust, could bolster the department's consistency of policy by providing policy alternatives that are realistic as well as effective. Civil rights administration, if applied uniformly, could assist ED in ensuring compliance. The discussion of the subject in the chapter highlighted the unique problems among and between other agencies with a similar Congressional mandate. The complaint processing system was discussed to pinpoint the inconsistency of policy and actual enforcement. The administrative factors identified explain the lack of uniformity of policy and enforcement in the Department of Education.

This information presents a strong case for the poor administration of the OCR. In addition, the administration of the regulatory function does have its problems, and the OCR could have done a better job. Given the fact that there havebeen different administrations over time, there have been variations from administration to administration; but overall the administrative function has remained the same.

CHAPTER IV

POLICY ENFORCEMENT AND AFFIRMATIVE ACTION

Generally, affirmative action has been successfully used as a device to remedy employment discrimination. In education, affirmative action has been used to remedy educational staff discrimination problems. Affirmative action will focus broad issues which relate to access to educational opportunity. This discussion will focus higher educational staff desegregation and the failure of OCR to effectively enforce the policy of desegregating educational staff.

Affirmative action as a method for remedying past discrimination has been debated continuously. ED's effort to enforce educational policy also has been plagued with additional problems as it relates to affirmative action. This chapter will identify factors that explain the Education Department's lack of uniformity of policy enforcement and affirmative action.

Any public educational institution which receives Federal financial assistance is required to comply with affirmative action guidelines to remedy past discrimination. Due to public controversy about affirmative action, the ED has not properly executed this function. With the grandiose role the federal government has initiated regarding educational policy since 1954, one can question the effectiveness. There are numerous Federal regulatory agencies which are effective in assuring compliance with Federal laws (i.e., Internal Revenue Service, National Labor Relations Board, etc.). During the period 1974-1982 there were many moves afoot in the Congress to pass legislation designed to further hinder compliance. These initiatives and bills will be discussed thoroughly in the next chapter.

Different arguments for affirmative action are discussed by notable commentators. This treatment reveals the public concern for and against the concept by various commentators. The Federal Government initially became involved in these issues in 1970 with Executive Order 11246, which is discussed later. Just as compliance has been ineffectual as demonstrated by *Adams*, so has the affirmative duty to remedy past discrimination. However, specific guidelines in 1972 were established by HEW; these guidelines will be discussed later. It is safe to say the same handicaps which affect compliance also affect affirmative action plans. This problem has many implications for higher education due to the historic exclusion of minorities and women. The latter part of the chapter reveals in detail the various guidelines, orders, and interpretations that exist in HEW to remedy past discrimination.

Given the problem with internal politics, especially the problems with the Office of General Counsel discussed in the last chapter, one can realize the complexity of internal confusion. The controversy over affirmative action has affected the Department due to social forces. These social forces can be divided generally into two groups. Civil rights groups, such as the SCLC, NAACP, and the Urban League, which have promoted affirmative action compose one group. The other group is not readily identifiable although there is a move to reinterpret the thrust of affirmative action. Recent court cases such as *Bakke* and *Weber* have given new direction to reinterpreting the meaning of the concept. Some believe the concept necessarily discriminates in reverse fashion. The old HEW efforts to eliminate past discrimination have also met challenges. The Walker amendment, which served as a rider to the Labor-HEW 1978 appropriations bill, which was not passed, would have served to hinder HEW's compliance activity. Under *Adams v. Califano* the HEW was ordered to enforce its desegregation guidelines. When viewing affirmative action enforcement, the data suggest the various degrees of complexity administrators were faced with in regulating in the public interest (A. Besner interview, October 28, 1980).

Affirmative action in the past years has been a very controversial issue in American society. In the study *The State of Black America: 1978*, the Urban League charged that the situation in the United States has grown worse and conditions will deteriorate unless "special arrangements" are made on behalf of Black Americans. The "special arrangements" can be accomplished through the efforts of an affirmative federal government sensitive and responsive to the needs of black Americans. As the 1970s ended, many efforts were being designed to forestall and curtail many of the advantages that Blacks and minorities received from affirmative action. With much of the controversy regarding affirmative action, scholars have researched and published articles critical of some of the efforts that support affirmative action.

Daniel P. Moynihan, in *Maximum Feasible Misunderstanding* (1969), criticized the efforts of the War on Poverty program and analyzed the elements of the program that doomed it to failure. Daniel Moynihan was criticized for a report he wrote in *The Negro Family* (1965) and for the controversial memo prepared for President Richard Nixon that recommended a period of "benign neglect" from the issues of race, prejudice, and bigotry.

In James S. Coleman's *Equal Opportunity Survey* (1966), commissioned by the Congress, it was brought out that issues not akin to race were responsible for limited educational opportunity structures. Nathan Glazer, in *Affirmative Discrimination* (1978), criticized school desegregation issues and the proposed resolution of problems of unequal schooling. Glazer also criticized affirmative action programs designed to alleviate discrimination for blacks.

Not only have white scholars turned their attention and analysis from race as a factor of limited opportunity, but black scholars as well addressed the declining significance of race. William Julius Wilson, Professor of Sociology at the University of Chicago, who published *The*

Declining Significance of Race (1970), maintains that, in modern industrial society, race is of less significance and class issues can effectively compete with race issues. However, he does not deny problems that middle-class blacks endure, but maintains that class is of more significance. Wilson summarizes his views this way:

> In the earlier periods, whether one focuses on the way race relations were structured by the economy, by the state or by both, racial oppression ranging from exploitation of Black labor by the economic elite to the elimination of Black competition, especially economic competition by the white masses, was a characteristic and important aspect of life. However..., in the modern industrial period the economy and the state have, in relatively independent ways, shifted the bases of racial antagonisms away from Black/White economic contact to social, political, and community issues. The net effect is a growing class division among Blacks. A situation, in other words, in which economic class has been elevated to a position of greater importance than that of race in determining individual black opportunities for living conditions and personal life experience. (1970, p. 47)

These statements summarize Wilson's views on the declining significance of race, and he maintains race is of less significance than class issues..

Thomas Sowell, a black economist at the University of California at Los Angeles, often writes on issues germane to Blacks. Sowell is highly critical of affirmative action programs. Sowell contends that blacks have suffered from the injury that "statistical representation" in jobs and access to education, is a grand fallacy the Black community has bought. Additionally, his analysis suggests that Blacks have not gained much from the affirmative action programs and these programs have given Blacks a false sense of accomplishment.

> The greatest dilemma in attempts to raise ethnic minority income is that those methods which have historically proved successful—self reliance, work skills, education, business experience—are all slow developing, while those methods which are direct and immediate—job quotas, charity, subsidies, preferential treatment—tend to undermine self-reliance and pride of achievement in the long run. (1980, p. 49)

This statement highlights Sowell's views on blacks and affirmative action wherein he suggests affirmative action programs give blacks a false sense of accomplishment.

In the area of school desegregation, many Black scholars have criticized the proposed strategies for remedying past discrimination. Many of the arguments center around questions of racial balance and the busing of students to achieve racial balance. Derrick A. Bell, a former NAACP attorney who has tried many school desegregation cases, contends: "There is simply too much evidence that integrated schools, even when achieved, do not bring either interracial understanding or academic improvement for poor Black children" (1980, p. 49).

Bell is currently a professor at the Harvard Law School. The problem in past school desegregation was with the strategies employed in that he no longer accepts the notion that integration was the only means of achieving equal educational opportunity. To understand the new shift in direction of many Black and white scholars who disagree with the methods and strategies of the movement of equality of opportunity, it might help to review the comments of Kenneth B. Clark. Clark is a social scientist who participated in the *Brown* decision by providing the Supreme Court with significant social science data. Clark found that segregated schools were inherently unequal. Clark used "dolls" in his study to reveal the reactions black students displayed for the black and white dolls. Clark contends that race is having increased significance even for middle-class Blacks due to school desegregation, affirmative action, and other programs. He affirms this fact by noting the white backlash to affirmative action issues. Clark further maintains that the backlash is promulgated by a "new brand" of sophisticated racists who are masquerading as liberals. In a recent symposium which discussed Bill Wilson's book *The Declining Significance of Race*, Clark stated:

> I must tell you quite candidly as I read what you write... I do think of ... Wattenberg, of Pat Moynihan, of that group that I in my counter-racist's way describe as "white neo-conservative liberals." Sometimes when I try to mask my racism, I call them the "Charles River Crew" using and exaggerating alleged racial progress (among what I still believe to be a very small portion of Blacks who have made it) to affect social policy.... Bill, what I'd like to see happen is for you to make it very, very clear that you are not to be associated with that "Charles River Crew" of sophisticated racists. (1980, p. 50)

These statements highlight Clarks views on Wilson's book *The Declining Significance of Race* and attempt to clarify the position of the author.

The debate over affirmative action and equal opportunity will continue, and there is not one analytical framework which will satisfy all observers. Additionally, the problems are so complex and rooted in every major institution in society, further study is necessary to make society equitable for its members. Murray Friedman, author of the *Commentary* article "The New Black

Intellectuals" (June 1980), has opinions that are different from this writer. Murray Friedman's analysis speaks to the fact that the new Black intellectuals are beginning to view problems of society in terms other than race and that race is not such a pervasive social phenomenon as previously conceived. This writer agrees in part, but also disagrees due to the fact, which Clark intimates, that only a few people of minority races have gained significant opportunity. Murray Friedman concludes:

> Overall, however, and despite their differences, what can be said about the new Black intellectuals is that in their individual voices and from their varying perspectives they have cast a harshly illuminating light on played-out analyses and policies of another era, while not neglecting the task of pointing out alternatives. This in itself, especially at a time when their white colleagues have been forced into mixedness, is a most welcome development. (1980, p. 51)

These ideas reveal Friedman's view on the new black intellectuals which he asserts have pointed to new and different analysis and policies of another era.

After reviewing current opposing views on affirmative action and equal opportunity, the stage is set for reviewing policies and practices in the Federal Government that relate to affirmative action in education. The concept of affirmative action, as applied, has received most success in business and industry during the period 1953-1981. In education, "academic freedom" rights have removed the university from the kind of regulations other social institutions have received. While some Blacks currently feel that they do not have their fair share of equal opportunity, some feel other groups will be vying for their slice of the American pie. Nevertheless, affirmative action is here and has been reaffirmed by the Supreme Court in *Steelworkers v. Weber, 443 U.S. 22 S.Ct. 2721, 61 L.Ed (1979)* and *University of California Regents v. Bakke, 438 U.S. 265 (1978).*

I. FEDERAL INVOLVEMENT IN AFFIRMATIVE ACTION

Federal involvement in the enforcement of affirmative action policies in higher education began in 1970 with a complaint filed by the Women's Equity Action League (WEAL), a women's civil rights group. The complaint alleged industry-wide discrimination against women in higher education. Prior to this action, the academic community was unfamiliar with any affirmative action remedies. The WEAL complaint was based on a Presidential Executive Order (11246) banning discrimination based on race, color, religion, and national origin. As stated earlier, prior to WEAL's action, the academic community had not become involved in any of these actions. Executive Order 11246, issued in 1970, stated that Federal contractors set clauses in their contracts banning discrimination based on race, color, national origin, and religion. In a subsequent order, No. 11375, sex was added to these requirements.

These Executive Orders are administered by the United States Department of Labor (DOL) and many other agencies to which DOL has delegated responsibility. When investigating discrimination cases involving educational institutions, ED-OCR forwards its findings in reports to the Secretary of Health, Education, and Welfare and the Secretary of the Department of Labor. In May of 1970 the Department of Labor issued Order 4, which required contractors to comply with the Executive Order in greater detail. In December of 1971, the Department of Labor issued revised Order 4 and required educational institutions with contracts of $50,000 or more to prohibit discrimination in their workforces. Under Revised Order 4, each Federal contractor was ordered to develop an affirmative action plan with goals and timetables for the hiring of women and minorities.

When an educational institution is investigated and found in non-compliance, the institution must "show cause" why sanction proceedings should not be initiated. Sometimes these proceedings can result in the termination of a Federal contract.

Prior to contract termination, the institution must have a hearing. The Office of Federal Contract Compliance Programs (OFCCP), a division of the Department of Labor, monitors Federal contracts awarded to educational institutions. Revised Order 4 required the delegation of enforcement responsibility to the HEW-OCR. There is also a memorandum of understanding between HEW and the Equal Employment Opportunity Commission (EEOC) giving EEOC authority to investigate those individual complaints that relate to employment discrimination as defined under Title VII of the Civil Rights Act. In 1972 HEW took responsibility and issued affirmative action guidelines. Those guidelines required goals and timetables not only for compliance but also for provisions that go beyond the prohibition of discrimination. To overcome the effects of past discrimination, these guidelines require employers to make special efforts to recruit, employ, and promote women and minorities. The guidelines read as follows:

> Nondiscrimination requires the elimination of all existing discriminatory conditions, whether purposeful or inadvertent.... *Affirmative action* requires the contractor to do more than ensure employment neutrality with regard to race, color, religion, sex, and national origin.... Affirmative action requires the employer to make additional efforts to recruit, employ and promote qualified members of groups formerly excluded, even if that exclusion cannot be traced to particular discriminatory actions on the part of the employer.... Revised Order

No. 4 requires a contractor to determine whether women and minorities are "underutilized" in its employee work force and, if that is the case, to develop as a part of its affirmative action program specific goals and timetables designed to overcome that underutilization.

... Underutilization is defined... as "having fewer women or minorities in a particular job that would reasonably be expected by their availability...."

If the contractor falls short of its goal at the end of the period it has set, that failure in itself does not require a conclusion of noncompliance. It does, however, require a determination by the contractor as to why the failure occurred....

Nothing in the Executive Order requires that a university contractor eliminate or dilute standards which are necessary to the successful performance of the institution's educational and research functions.

At a later point the *Guidelines* provide more specifically for the development of goals and timetables.... (U.S. Dept. HEW, 1972, pp. 2-3)

The *Guidelines* assume the availability of minorities and women if a Federal contractor does not already have an equal representation of minorities and women in his workforce. This denotes that underutilization exists—thus, noncompliance. The goals and timetables included in the affirmative action plans speak to "reasonable" methods of ensuring compliance. After goals and timetables are set, then it is necessary to make a comparison between the current workforce and available data. For example, if a university is developing an affirmative action plan in accordance with availability data obtained from the Department of Labor (which reveals the percentages of minorities and women in the Standard Metropolitan Statistical Area [SMSA]), then all job classifications in the university must reflect the availability of minorities and women in the Standard Metropolitan Statistical Area

In many institutions the appropriate unit for goals is the school or division, rather than the department. While estimates of availability in academic employment can best be determined on a disciplinary basis, anticipated turnover and vacancies can usually be calculated on a wider basis. While a school, division or college may be the organizational unit which assumes responsibility for setting and achieving goals, departments which have traditionally excluded women or minorities from their ranks are expected to make particular efforts to recruit, hire and promote women and minorities. In other words, the Office for Civil Rights will be concerned not only with whether a school meets its overall goals, but also whether apparent general success has been achieved only by strenuous efforts on the part of a few departments. (Carnegie Council on Policy Studies in Higher Education, 1975, p. 118)

These statements highlight the appropriate application of affirmative action in colleges and universities and points out the OCR's concern for departmental efforts to establish goals and timetables.

However, many of the OCR's enforcement activities are related to Revised Order 4 rather than its own guidelines. Information relating to OCR negotiations with the University of California at Berkeley revealed that where underutilization is found, the OCR makes a literal interpretation of the order. Each and every unit or department within the university must develop goals and timetables to remedy the underutilization. The period for future compliance is generally five years; however, sometimes compliance can be ensured within a three-to-five-year period.

II. GOALS, QUOTAS, AND QUALIFICATIONS

Finally, it is important to note the distinction between goals, quotas, and qualifications. The Federal establishment makes a clear distinction between those terms. One of the problems with effective administration is that educational institutions may administer programs which make no such distinction. A related issue is the "most qualified" or sometimes the "best qualified." Generally, there are three alternatives that are operative:

1) "Most qualified" may be determined on strictly academic grounds alone—knowledge of the subject and ability to teach it and add to it.

2) It may be judged on broader grounds of overall contributions, including where appropriate, the ability to serve effectively as "models" and "mentors" to women and minority students.

3) It may be considered loosely as being whatever is most suitable in meeting the established goals. Many variations exist within and among these three major alternatives (Carnegie Council on Policy Studies in Higher Education, 1975, p. 129)

The American Association of University Professors (AAUP) favors the second alternative. The report of the Commission on Discrimination of the AAUP expressed this general point of view in the following terms:

> We would go further to say that special efforts to attract persons to improve the overall diversity of a faculty, and to broaden it specifically from its unisex or unirace sameness, seem to us to state a variety of affirmative action which deserves encouragement. The argument to the special relevance of race and sex as qualifying characteristics draws its strength from a recognition of the richness which a variety of intellectual perspectives and life experiences can bring to the educational program. It is more than simply a matter of providing jobs for persons from groups which have in the past been unfairly excluded from an opportunity to compete for t hem; it is a matter of reorganizing the academic institution to fulfill its basic commitment to those whoa re seriously concerned to maintain the academic enterprise as a vital social force. (1973, pp. 180-181)

These ideas represent some of the AAUP's perspectives on affirmative action which support the concept and the role of the academic institution in these matters.

Other types of goals, timetables, and qualifications are related to applicant pools. The applicant pool concept is applied to different universities in different manners. Generally, research universities give more consideration at the initial appointment stage, whereas other requirements are applied in faculty tenure situations. Often the university, when under investigation for discrimination, claimed exemption from Federal regulations based on the Federal investigators' failure to apply the regulations to the university environment. Specifically, professors in certain disciplines claimed that only experts or people with the credentials or training could identifiy the characteristics necessary for selection of faculty. In a particular case, this argument failed to withstand scrutiny, and the investigator proceeded with the case based on the established theories of discrimination that are not based on subjective criteria developed as a subterfuge (Interview with Equal Opportunity Specialist James Jordan, July 8, 1980).

III. AFFIRMATIVE ACTION AND HIGHER EDUCATION

There are many issues that relate to affirmative action in higher education which address policies and practices designed to assist minorities and women. The Women's Equity Action

League (WEAL) was successful in the action it brought in 1970. On the other hand, Blacks have not fared so well with their efforts to overcome comprehensive discrimination, and their actions do not have as broad a base as the WEAL action.

> Perhaps no single procedure to eliminate inequality in hiring in higher education has surfaced the attitudes, fears, anxieties, and bigoted behavior of academicians as has the affirmative action concept. Affirmative action is considered by many white males in the academic community to be the "enfant terrible" of all governmental involvement in higher education and is to be resisted at all cost. Black educators of both sexes tell us that, regardless of their qualifications, this plan is the only vehicle they have left to gain entry into the faculty and administrative ranks of predominantly white institutions. The vehicle is not an effective one; we are told that the federal government must enforce it to make it work. (Moore and Wagstaff, 1974, pp. 72, 73)

The above ideas reveal the perceptions of Moore and Wagstaff on affirmative action which support the view blacks have not fared well in efforts to overcome comprehensive discrimination.

Given the foregoing discussion, it is evident that the time is ripe for Black Americans to participate in all aspects of higher education. Since the *Plessy v. Ferguson* doctrine of "separate but equal," Black educators in higher education have been employed primarily by traditionally Black colleges. There was a backlash from white educators, who felt that unqualified Blacks would be hired by white institutions and thus affect the quality of education in those institutions. The affirmative action guidelines were condemned by many educators such as Sidney Hook of New York University, John Bunzel, President of San Jose State University, and Paul Seaburg of the University of California at Berkeley, who again asserted the notion that hiring unqualified Blacks would occur (Goodman, 1972).

IV. REACTION TO AFFIRMATIVE ACTION

Initially, the academic reaction to affirmative action of Blacks and women was one of resistance. Robert Perrins puts in this way: "The Federal government has been slow in realizing that employment descriptions and practices in an institution of higher education are not as easily quantifiable as, say, those in an automobile plant" (1972). Again, much resistance has come from educational institutions as they address past inequities in education. Generally, educational institutions have been innovators. Much social change has stemmed from movements embraced by students and faculty which had their genesis on college campuses. Despite these innovative change-oriented thrusts generated on college campuses, resistance to change has been embodied in educational institutions. Moore and Wagstaff (1974) assert:

> Although administrators are often charged with the responsibility for racial discrimination in higher education institutions, in reality they are frequently the scapegoats, defenders rather than perpetrators of the unlawful and illegal practices. (p. 74)

The Committee on Discrimination of the AAUP recognizes that:

> In too many cases it is the faculty itself, or a significant portion of it, which has opposed change in such areas as appointment policies. Improperly utilizing the principle of preserving quality, faculty members responsible for recommending appointments have denied entrance to the academy to women and to persons of minority race and background. Faculties have likewise been influenced by existing patterns which lead to discrimination based on improper considerations in such matters as salary, retention, promotion, and service on decision-making bodies (1974, p. 91)

Moore and Wagstaff suggest a sophisticated strategy of non-compliance is designed to oppose the selection of Black faculty. They state that just as public school officials use the "all deliberate speed" language and the other loopholes in the 1954 *Brown* decision to evade the spirit of the decision to implement or oppose it according to their own proposals, timetables, and desires, so college administrators, supported by the professoriate, use the "Every good faith" language and loopholes of Order No. 4 of the Department of Labor to evade implementation of Executive Order 11246. Since 1974 this writer believes there has been enhanced representation of minority and female faculty and staff. However, it is also believed there are pockets or resistance.

This chapter has discussed the Department of Education's effort to enforce equal education policy, featuring its related problem of affirmative action. The factors identified explain the department's activities and requirements as they relate to educational policy and affirmative action. The proper role of the Federal Government in affirmative action forces HEW to develop and follow its orders and guidelines. Various dimensions of goals, quotas, and qualifications have made the ED's problem of affirmative action in higher education especially complex. Lastly, the reaction to affirmative action by interest groups has been a factor which explains inconsistent policy enforcement in the department.

In conclusion, the current reaction to affirmative action by interest groups such as WEAL and the NAACP reveals a lack of enforcement by the Education Department. Since an affirmative action plan is designed to effect change over a three- to five-year period of time, compliance must be reviewed periodically.

> In 1980 the U.S. Commission on Civil Rights informed top Carter administration equal opportunity officials that its researchers had found the data virtually useless in assessing the effects of affirmative action in given organizations since 1973, according to interoffice corespondence. (*Washington Post*, April 12, 1982, p. A10)

Due to a lack of current hard data, it is difficult to measure the effects of affirmative action enforcement since 1973. However, we do know HEW developed its guidelines in October of 1972, and it is doubtful that total compliance was effected in one year.

CHAPTER V

THE CONGRESS AND SCHOOL DESEGREGATION

Various Congressional actions have made the Department of Education's enforcement effort complex and ineffective. Factors will be analyzed for their possible effects on the Department of Education's compliance function. These factors also explain some of the reasons for the ED's inconsistent enforcement of school desegregation policy.

As the Department of Education pursues its compliance responsibilities under the Civil Rights Act, the department also has to respond to different constraints placed on the department by the Congress. Certain actions in the Congress have complicated matters and produced the inconsistent policy enforcement identified in the chapter "Federal Government Enforcement and the *Adams* Litigation."

There have been numerous bills and amendments initiated in the Congress designed to limit the old HEW's enforcement of Titles VI and VI. All of these bills and amendments were not passed. These bills are anti-civil rights riders to appropriation bills (Leadership Conference on Civil Rights, October 10, 1980). When funds are appropriated to regulatory agencies, these bills would prohibit certain practices by the agency. This discussion reveals the inherent problems involved with the enforcement of educational policy. Onesignificant problem that exists is the HEW mandate to enforce compliance with *Adams* and the constraints placed on the agency by the Eagleton-Biden amendment passed in 1978.

The Eagleton-Biden amendment, which was upheld in the courts, prohibited HEW from administratively requiring busing to achieve school desegregation. Given the apparent inconsistencies in the government's enforcement effort to ensure equal educational opportunity, it is necessary that combined efforts be coordinated among t he three branches. After viewing the actions in the Congress, the discretionary defense of the agency can perhaps be supported in some instances. The anti-civil rights riders to appropriation bills have been initiated by representatives responding to their constituencies. These riders, in some instances, develop serious constitutional questions. The Dornan-Ashbrook amendment to H.R. 7583, which was an appropriations rider, would have limited and constrained the Internal Revenue Service (IRS) from formulating or enforcing any regulation that would deny a tax exemption to a private school that discriminates. This amendment passed the House and was up for Senate action in the 97th Congress (1st session). The amendment did not pass in the conference committee. In view of the landmark case *Brown v. Board of Education*, the efforts to eliminate the dual system of education and discrimination are documented. The anti-civil rights riders to appropriations bills set the stage for resistance to previous law in violation of the *Brown* decision.

In 1964 there was much reaction to the Federal Government in the form of civil-rights marches and demonstrations. The Johnson administration's War on Poverty redirected efforts to remedy civil rights problems (Spring, 1978). This was done by placing emphasis on the public school and using the school as a vehicle to remedy the past inequities of minorities (Spring, 1978). The War on Poverty programs are often criticized, and currently politicians are still seeking answers to social problems and poverty. There were alternatives to this course of action; however, the government chose the public school as the vehicle to remedy the effects of poverty. Ironically, less than 20 years later the same Congress which passed the Civil Rights Act (1964) is posing different bills and enacting into law very different types of legislation. Again, the coordination of education policy and enforcement is necessary in order for the federal government to maintain one position on these matters. The situation is characterized by the Judicial branch promotion of one approach, the Executive branch a different approach, and the Congressional branch yet another.

Often Congress through its committees can influence agency policy by taking direct action with agency department heads. Since 1976 Congress has proposed and adopted several amendments which have inhibited the Department of Health, Education, and Welfare's Office of Civil Rights from its mission to enforce the desegregation laws. The amendments and proposed legislation have impacted the Office of Civil Rights (OCR), placing OCR between complying with Presidential directives transmitted to agency chiefs and Congressional inquiries, which include policies designed to further forestall the agency's enforcement efforts. Numerous types of legislation have been introduced for the purpose of prohibiting, restricting, and excluding the Office of Civil Rights from enforcing compliance with civil rights laws. These pieces of legislation will be documented, their legislative history briefly discussed, and the possible effects of these bills and amendments on civil rights enforcement will be analyzed.

I. RESTRICTION ON STUDENT TRANSPORTATION CONTAINED IN THE LABOR-HEW APPROPRIATIONS ACT (EAGLETON-BIDEN)

None of the funds contained in this Act shall be used to require, directly or indirectly, the transportation of any student to a school other than the school which is nearest the student's home, except for a student requiring special education, to the school offering such special education in order to comply with Title VI of the Civil Rights Act of 1964. For the purpose of this section an indirect requirement of transportation of students includes the transportation of students to carry out a plan involving the reorganization of the grade structure of schools, the pairing of schools, or the clustering of shools, or any combination of grade restructuring, pairing, or clustering. The prohibition described in this section does not include the establishment of magnet schools.

This provision is known as the "Eagleton-Biden" amendment and has been contained in the Labor-HEW appropriations bills since fiscal year 1978. The amendment has its origin in the "Byrd" amendment to the 1976 and 1977 Labor-HEW appropriations bills. The Byrd amendment would have prohibited HEW from requiring transportation of any student beyond the school nearest the student's home in order to comply with Title VI of the Civil Rights Act of 1964. The Byrd Amendment did not pass in the conference committees in 1976 and 1977. Under this interpretation, traditional desegregation techniques such as pairing or clustering of schools or grade restructuring could only be applied in working out a desegregation plan before the busing restriction was applied. HEW's interpretation of the Byrd amendment was upheld by Attorney General Griffin Bell.

Due to the HEW-Justice interpretation of the Byrd amendment, the House and Senate agreed to the stricter language contained in the Eagleton-Biden amendment. While the Carter Administration opposed Eagleton-Biden, efforts to delete and revise it were unsuccessful. The most recent effort to revise Eagleton-Biden was an amendment presented to the 1980 Labor-HEW appropriations committee by Senator Paul Tsongas (*Cong. Rec.* S 9959, July 20, 1979). It would have replaced Eagleton-Biden with language contained in the 1976 and 1977 appropriations bills (Byrd). However, the Tsongas bill was rejected by the Senate on July 20, 1979. Senator Brooke, an opponent of the bill, stated that it would have denied HEW all other means of achieving desegregation (121 *Cong. Rec.* S 16540, September 23, 1975).

The intent of Senator Tsongas' bill was to amend Eagleton-Biden and prevent HEW from enforcing Title VI of the Civil Rights Act of 1964. Under the bill, HEW's Office of Civil

Rights (OCR) would have been precluded from requiring school districts found in violation of Eagleton-Biden from desegregating their schools through changes in existing grade structure or by relocating particular grades, whenever transportation past the school nearest the student's home was involved.

Consequently, HEW was unable to recommend that school districts found in violation of Title VI implement grade reorganization plans involving transportation. This remained the case where students awaiting assignments or reassignments were being transported and the transportation resulting from the grade reorganization would have been less than that previously provided. This amendment was supported by parents and communities who opposed forced busing, these parent groups pressured their Congressmen into backing the bill.

The imposition of a transportation limitation on HEW before a remedy had been proposed conflicted with Title VI. Reorganization of grade structures are pairing or clustering of schools had been used for years, and such techniques had long been recognized by the Federal courts as a permissible elimination of past desegregation. Moreover, in passing the Education Amendments of 1974, Congress authorized the revision of school attendance zones or grade structures to correct past inequities in equal educational opportunity. This section of the statute, commonly referred to as the Esch Amendment, was included in Title II of the Education Amendments of 1974 (P.L. 93-380, 88 Stat. 494) and enacted in August 1974. Under the Esch Amendment, HEW, in considering the acceptability of these proposed plans to correct violations of Title VI, is required to prioritize its list of remedies. Naturally, this is a difficult, tedious, and involved process which impedes the effective enforcement of the agency's compliance activities.

ED applies the remedies provided by statute only after determining that an existing student assignment practice is unlawfully and intentionally discriminatory. Each in such instances, limitations are imposed on the type of additional transportation that may be utilized to carry out the desegregation plan. Transportation was limited to schools which are "closer or next closest" to a student's place of residence and which offer the student the appropriate grade level and type of education. In *Swann v. Charlotte-Mecklenburg Board of Education, 402 U.S. 1 (1971).* the Supreme Court held that school systems were not required to bus students when the time and distance involved were so great as to impair the health of students or significantly impinge on the educational process.

The actions permitted under the Eagleton-Biden Act have little, if anything, to do with Title VI's remedies for unconstitutional discrimination. The amendment authorized HEW to require plans necessitating transportation of students to special education classes. Such classes, held in particular schools located beyond the nearest school to a student's home, would have little, if any, effect upon desegregation. Furthermore, the amendment would permit HEW to require school districts to establish magnet schools irrespective of a student's need for transportation beyond the nearest schools—a practice that has rarely resulted in effective desegregation. In theory, the magnet school concept was viable; but, in practice, the concept did not solve desegregation problems, although it impacted these problems in a variety of ways.

Experience has demonstrated that the Esch provision severely restricted HEW's authority to remedy unconstitutional educational discrimination involving student transportation. The Act's restrictions discouraged school districts from voluntarily complying with Title VI. When these districts refuse to achieve appropriate desegregation remedies, HEW must refer the cases to the Department of Justice for court action. Such referrals result in delayed compliance by prolonging enforcement and bypassing the administrative processes created by Congress under Title IV. In *Brown v. Califano*, the NAACP Legal Defense Fund challenged the constitutionality of the Eagleton-Biden amendment. On July 18, 1978, the U.S. District Court for the District of Columbia upheld the Act's constitutionality as long as HEW continued to refer transportation cases to the Department of Justice for litigation.

II. BILL TO LIMIT AUTHORITY OF FEDERAL COURTS TO ORDER STUDENT TRANSPORTATION (ROTH-BIDEN)

S. 228 was introduced by Senator William Roth (for himself and Senator Joseph Biden) on January 25, 1979. The bill was referred to the Senate Committee on the Judiciary, Subcommittee on the Constitution; but no action was taken.

An identical bill, H.R. 1661, was introduced by Representative Thomas Evans on January 31, 1979. This bill was referred to the House Committee on the Judiciary, subcommittee on Courts, Civil Liberties, and the Administration of Justice; but again no action was taken.

S. 228 is virtually identical to a bill that Senators Roth and Biden introduced on June 9, 1977. That bill, S. 1651, was the subject of hearings held by the House Committee on the Judiciary on June 15-16 and July 21-22, 1977. It was revised on September 21, 1977 (Senate Report No. 95-443) and then reintroduced as an amendment by Senator Roth (for himself and Biden, Bartlett, Hayakawa, Schweiker, DeConcini, and Chiles) to S. 1753, a bill to extend the Elementary and Secondary Education Act of 1965 (*Cong. Rec.* S. 14079, August 23, 1978). The Senate agreed to table the amendment on August 23, 1978 (49 yeas to 47 nays).

This amendment would have seriously restricted the authority of the Federal courts to remedy racial segregation in schools by prohibiting the Federal courts from ordering transportation of students unless the court had first determined that a discriminatory purpose had motivated the violation. In addition, when ordering the busing of students, the courts should order no more extensive relief than was necessary to adjust the student racial composition of schools to reflect what it would have been without any constitutional violations. Roth-Biden also required written findings by the court in such cases as to the discriminatory purpose of each violation and the degree to which the concentration by race, color, or national origin in particular schools varied from what it would have been had no such violation occurred. The bill stayed implementation of any Federal court order requiring interdistrict transportation until all judicial appeals were exhausted.

Attorney General Griffin Bell found the Roth-Biden bill undesirable and possibly unconstitutional. The undesirable sections required a finding of discriminatory purpose before ordering particular remedies, limited remedies ordered to only those "essential" to repair denial of equal educational opportunity, and restated the current case law and Congressional restrictions. Some of the provisions, like determining that a discriminatory purpose in education was the "principal motivating factor" would have unnecessarily complicated evidentiary fact gathering in school desegregation litigation. Other provisions would have generated substantial litigation resulting in delayed enforcement of court injunctions banning such violations. This is contrary to past Supreme Court decisions which held that the process of school desegregation should no longer be delayed (*Alexander v. Holmes County, 396 U.S. 19 [1969]; Green v. Board of Education of New Kent County, 191 U.S. 430 [1968]* and *flies in the face of the catchwords of the Brown* decision, "with all deliberate speed." Attorney General Bell sent a letter to the Senate Committee on the Judiciary on S 1651 (Roth-Biden), which stated that the Department of Health, Education, and Welfare had concurred with his opinion.

The bill presupposed that school desegregation involving the transportation of students was objectionable; therefore, the bill would encourage endless litigation before any remedial actions were imposed, even though constitutional violations had clearly been established. Congress firmly opposed the conveying of that message. Rather than encourage communities to develop constructive approaches to resolve disputes involving school desegregation, S. 228 would have permitted communities opposing desegregation access to the Federal courts, thus supporting a "litigation forever" opposition strategy. Such strategy was a clever, but costly, method of preventing and stalling desegregation efforts. Yet simple "stall tactics" have had deleterious effects on desegregation efforts; furthermore, such tactics perpetuate the maintenance of unlawful dual systems.

III. AMENDMENT TO LIMIT AUTHORITY OF THE DEPARTMENT OF JUSTICE IN SCHOOL DESEGREGATION CASES (COLLINS)

No part of any appropriation contained in this Act shall be used by the Department of Justice to bring any sort of action to require directly or indirectly the transportation of any student to a school other than the school which is nearest the student's home, except for a student requiring special education as a result of being mentally or physically handicapped.

The amendment was first introduced by Representative James Collins to the Department of Justice Appropriation Authorization for Fiscal Year 1979 (*Cong. Rec.* H 10793, September 26, 1978). The amendment was adopted by the House on September 26, 1978, but deleted in Conference Committee.

Later Representative Collins introduced an amendment identical to HR 4892, a bill making appropriations for the Departments of State, Justice, Commece, the Judiciary, and related agencies for fiscal year 1980 (*Cong. Rec.* H 5839, July 12, 1979). The House adopted Collins' amendment on July 12, 1979. Senator Jesse Helms had offered the "Collins" amendment during Senate consideration of H.R. 4392 (*Cong. Rec.* S 10423, July 24, 1979), but the amendment was rejected by the Senate and subsequently deleted in Conference Committee. The Collins amendment would have seriously interfered with the ability of the Department of Justice to insure that no Federal funds would support unconstitutional school segregation. It would also have interfered with the authority of the Department of Justice to protect the rights of minority students seeking equal educational opportunity.

The Collins amendment incorrectly assumed that the Justice Department brought legal actions only to require student transportation. This assumption was incorrect as the sole enforcement authority of the Department of Justice regarding school desegregation was to bring civil actions under one of the Congressional enactments prohibiting racial discrimination (e.g., Title VI, Title IV). The Justice Department had no authority to require transportation or any other remedy for correcting illegal segregation. It was the Federal Judiciary alone that determined violations and ordered appropriate remedies. The Justice Department merely litigated matters deemed unconstitutional.

In cases where transportation may have been required to correct discriminatory student assignment practices, the amendment precluded judicial relief. This raised grave constitutional questions, when viewed in light of current Congressional restrictions on student transportation contained in the Labor-HEW Appropriations Act (Eagleton-Biden). Collins also prohibited

HEW from requiring school districts to transport a student beyond the nearest school, a procedure that might have been necessary after viewing the community profile. As a result, HEW had no recourse but to refer desegregation cases to the Justice Department when transportation was involved and a school district refused to voluntarily comply with Title VI of the Civil Rights Act of 1964 by adopting an acceptable desegregation plan. In effect, this amendment would have removed the litigation alternative when a noncomplying school district refused to negotiate a desegregation plan with HEW.

Again, the NAACP Legal Defense Fund challenged the constitutionality of the Eagleton-Biden amendment in *Brown v. Califano*. On July 18, 1978, the U.S. District Court for the Distsrict of Columbia held that the provision was constitutional so long as HEW could refer cases requiring transportation to Justice for litigation. For this reason, it was appropriate to advise a school district that the matter would be referred to the Department of Justice if the district did not voluntarily develop an acceptable plan. This approach reconciled the Eagleton-Biden amendment with the constitutional obligation of the Government not to provide funds to segregated school districts. The decision was tempered by the statement that the holding applied only to the *prima facie* constitutionality of the provision, and the plaintiffs could seek further relief if the litigation alternative proved unworkable. The Department of Justice's views on the Collins amendment were expressed in a letter, dated July 17, 1979, to the Senate Committee on Appropriations. In 1971 the Supreme Court ruled in *Swann v. Charlotte-Mecklenburg Board of Education, 402 U.S. 1 (1971)*, that transportation was a permissible tool to correct unconstitutional school segregation. That decision was reaffirmed when the Supreme Court decided the *Dayton Board of Education v. Brinkman* case and the *Colulmbus Board of Education v. Penick* case (July 2, 1979). Thus, the Collins Amendment was inconsistent with these Supreme Court holdings.

IV. AMENDMENT TO PROHIBIT ANY TIMETABLE, GOAL, RATIO, QUOTA, OR NUMERICAL REQUIREMENT IN HIRING AND ADMISSIONS PRACTICES (WALKER)

None of the funds appropriated in this Act may be obligated or expended in connection with the issuance, implementation, or enforcement of any rule, regulation, standard, guideline, recommendation, or order issued by the Secretary of Health, Education, and Welfare which for purposes of compliance with any timetable, goal, ratio, quota, or other numerical requirement related to race, creed, color, national origin, or sex requires any individual or entity to take any action with respect to (1) the hiring or promotion policies or practices of such individual or entity, or (2) the admissions policies or practices of such individual or entity.

The amendment was introduced by Representative Robert Walker to the fiscal year 1978 Labor-HEW appropriations bill (*Cong. Rec.* H 6099, June 17, 1977). The House agreed to a substitute amendment introduced by Representative Elliot Levitas that deleted the words "timetable" and "goal" (*Cong. Rec.* H 6102, June 17, 1977), but the Conference Committee ignored Levitas' substitute amendment. The Walker amendment was introduced by Senators Samuel Hayakawa and Jesse Helms to the fiscal year 1978 Labor-HEW appropriations bill (*Cong. Rev.* S 10029, July 20, 1979).

The Senate agreed to a substitute amendment introduced by Senator Jacob Javits limited to a prohibition against any "quota" regarding admission to an institution of higher education (*Cong. Rec.* S 10033, July 20, 1979), but again the conference Committee deleted the substitute amendment. The provision was directed at the issuance and enforcement of certain civil rights requirements relating to the employment and admissions policies and practices of recipients of Federal funds and Federal contracts. Clearly, the key words to the provision were "for purposes of compliance with any timetable, goal, ratio, quota, or other numerical requirement related to race, creed, color, national origin or sex."

It was unclear what specific civil rights enforcement activities were intended to be prohibited by the Walker amendment; however, its effect could have been: (1) to prohibit HEW from requiring certain types of remedial action by recipients found to be in violation of nondiscrimination laws, such as Title VI of the Civil Rights Act of 1964 (prohibiting discrimination on the basis of race, color, national origin in Federal-assisted programs) and Title IX of the Education Amendments of 1972 (prohibiting discrimination on the basis of sex in Federally assisted education programs); and (2) to prevent the Department from complying with court orders (such as *Adams v. Califano*) which require the Department to issue and enforce desegregation guidelines. It would have prohibited HEW from enforcing its guidelines on affirmative action.

Section 408 of the Public Law 94-482 prohibited HEW from deferring or limiting Federal assistance

on the basis of any failure to comply with the imposition of quotas (or any other numerical requirements which have the effect of imposing quotas) on student admissions practices or an institution of higher education or community college receiving Federal assistance.

The Department did not impose quotas on student admissions; therefore, Section 408 has not altered HEW policy. Although the Walker amendment was broader, it applied not only to "quotas" but to "timetables, goals, ratios, or other numerical requirements." It affected not only colleges or universities, but any " individual or entity"; and it covered employment practices as well as student admissions policies. It appears Walker would have had an impact on the Equal Employment Opportunity Commission's (EEOC) compliance activities.

The Walter amendment could have been construed as prohibiting HEW from applying or enforcing goals and timetables which have been traditional methods widely used by educational institutions and by other recipients of Federal funds to remedy discrimination against minorities and women in employment and education. Prohibition on the use of goals and timetables would prevent HEW from enforcing civil rights laws by requiring funded institutions to adopt and implement effective remedies for discrimination. HEW also used this method to determine an institution's compliance with the agency's voluntary affirmative action programs. HEW's goals were not necessarily rigid or arbitrary quotas. When an educational institution agreed to correct a discriminatory practice by setting a goal, the institution pledged "good faith" efforts and attempted to reach its objective within a certain period of time. As long as the institution took effective measures to achieve that goal, it would not be found in violation of the civil rights laws. However, under a remedial plan that provided for goals and timetables, there were no requirements that an institution hire or admit unqualified individuals.

The language "ratio... or other numerical requirement" also presented problems, if the language was broadly interpreted to limit the types of remedies that are applied to correct the present effects of past practices of discrimination in employment and education. For instance, an employer may be required to adopt a corrective plan that encompasses the term "ratio," even though such a remedy is in essence "a goal" to employ a certain number of qualified women and/ or minorities. A ratio is a tool frequently used to determine or express an appropriate goal or as an indicator to gauge progress in meeting particular goals.

Although the Department does not impose quotas on student admissions, higher education institutions are required by Title VI to correct the effects of any past discrimination in their admissions policies. In the previous chapter, under an order issued by the U.S. District Court for the District of Columbia in the case of *Adams v. Califano*, HEW was required to issue criteria specifying the ingredients of an acceptable Title VI desegregation plan for six state higher education systems. The court held that "specific commitments [were necessary] for a workable higher education plan... concerning admission, recruitment, and retention of students." Consistent with the court order, HEW's desegregation guidelines called for the institutions to get goals and timetables for accomplishing desegregation. The desegregation plans that HEW negotiated with five state systems of higher education provided for goals and timetables and was in direct conflict with the Walker amendment and HEW's obligations under *Adams v. Califano*. Presumably, under Walker, HEW would not be able to enforce the desegregation commitments made by the higher education institutions or require an appropriate remedy in cases where institutions failed to remedy the harmful present effects of past discrimination. The issuance of guidelines specifying acceptable desegregation plans was developed in response to HEW's lax enforcement of Title VI of the Civil Rights Act.

It is unclear whether the Walker amendment's reference to "the admissions policies or practices of such individual or entity" is applicable to elementary and secondary school student assignments as well as to admissions to higher education institutions. If it applies to the former, the amendment could restrict the Department's authority to remedy illegal school segregation under Title VI. Such an interpretation of the amendment could also effect the Department's authority to rectify other practices of segregation within schools. But the language of the Walker amendment may confuse higher education institutions and other recipients of HEW funds as to the types of remedies that are required to correct past discrimination. Furthermore, by enacting Walker, Congress would have subjected institutions to standards that differ from those imposed by the courts in constitutional cases.

This chapter reviewed various actions in the Congress that relate to school desegregation and equal opportunity in education. The various amendments and bills discussed placed severe constraints on the agency.

During the period 1974-1980 the Esch and Eagleton-Biden amendments actually effected the OCR's compliance effort (they were the only initiatives which passed both houses); however, the subsequent initiatives and the climate in which they were introduced actually affected what the compliance agency could do to enforce the law. The same Congress that introduced legislation and confirms cabinet members also sought to direct the department's enforcement practices. Being aware of these activities, the department's officials used their discretion in their perceived best interest. Again, during the period 1973-1981 the department was under the court order in *Adams* to enforce the law. As the federal department enforces equal opportunity in education, a lack of coordination and direction exists. These factors explain the reasons for inconsistent policy enforcement.

CHAPTER VI

POLITICS OF FEDERAL POLICY

This chapter will discuss the political influences that cause a lack of uniformity of policy and enforcement. The chapter cites presidential leadership, congressional initiative, and client-oriented groups as the major influencing political factors which impact on Federal policy. When considering political forces affecting the Department of Education during the period 1954 to 1981, it is important to understand how politics can effect educational policy in school desegregation issues. Politics in this paper is defined as the competition between and among competing interest groups for power and leadership. Power and control in educational policy making are viewed from two perspectives: first, the formal policy-making process, whereby the President, Congress, and Federal agencies exert influence and control over policy; and second, the groups outside government that provide information that can influence Federal education policy (Spring, 1978).

I. PRESIDENTIAL LEADERSHIP

At the national level, educational policy making is wrought with politics. Politics provides for power and control in making Federal education policy. Politics is viewed from the formal policy-making process whereby the President, Congress, and Federal agencies exert influence and control over policy.

A great deal of the activity of this federal government in education since the 1950s can be explained in terms of presidential politics. Traditionally, American presidents have not given a great deal of attention to educational matters because education has been considered a state and local matter and because other domestic and foreign problems have taken precedence over educational issues. But beginning in the 1950s, American presidents have been able to confront educational problems directly because of national and international events. For instance, President Eisenhower during the early years of his administration did not make education one of the focuses of his administration. In fact, he refused to discuss the 1954 Supreme Court decision (*Brown v. Board of Education of Topeka*) with regard to school desegregation. In his autobiography, *Waging Peace, 1956-1961*, he stated that he felt the Civil Rights campaign was an attempt to cause him to lose political support in the presidential election of 1956. (Spring, 1978, p. 157)

The statements highlight actions in the federal government which can be explained in terms of politics. The statements also reflect the influence or lack thereof in education matters on behalf of the Executive branch. Just as a president's actions can have a bearing on educational policy, his ignorance of educational issues can also adversely affect his election or re-election. When educational issues involve civil rights matters, the problem can place an added burden on the president. Presidential leadership is important in political action affecting the HEW-OCR. Unlike President Eisenhower, President Kennedy promoted civil rights interests. Kennedy emphasized civil rights as a major policy in his administration, although two years into his term the progress in civil rights was slow. As stated previously, many black Americans became discontent with Kennedy's progress in civil rights. However, John F. Kennedy became the first president to make aid to education a significant component of his domestic policy program (Spring, 1978, p. 157).

Under President Johnson, more civil rights gains were made. Though it appeared President Johnson was a friend to civil rights, it was the social forces that prompted the president's involvement in these matters. During President Johnson's administration, the HEW-OCR came into being. As the "equal opportunity" theme prevailed, President Johnson viewed education as a significant part of his "War on Poverty" program (Spring, 1972, p. 157).

President Nixon's thrust during his administration viewed civil rights from a "benign neglect" perspective. The president felt too much attention had been given to issues of civil rights:

Mr. Nixon would have a difficult time extracting a high priority for education from a budget that had so little flexibility possible in fiscal year 1973, and which also overlapped with a presidential election year. With regard to the budget, Mr. Nixon found his budgetary options to be more constrained than those which faced his predecessors in the early sixties.

At the same time that the administration has proposed revenue sharing (emergency aid to desegregating districts having been enacted) it has also been cautiously preserving its combined deferral same-maintenance-level direction.

In keeping with this direction, the equal opportunity proposals of the president in the spring of 1972 would combine ESEA Title I and Emergency School Assistance funding to provide limited resources of $300 per "deprived child." (Hughes and Hughes, 1972, p. 193)

These statements highlight President Nixon's ideas on civil rights enforcement and document this lack of budgetary priority for education.

Though school desegregation continued to be an explosive issue, President's Ford, Carter, and Reagan failed to significantly discuss it in their presidential campaigns. The Reagan administration attempted to abolish the newly formed Education Department, founded under the Carter administration. President Carter, like Johnson, supported civil rights enforcement and led the HEW-OCR's role in ensuring compliance. While the department was under court order in *Adams*, the newly appointed Secretary for Education, Shirley Hufstedler, complied with the court by "signing off" on documents, keeping in step with the court order's time frames. Under the Reagan administration, Secretary Terrell Bell was not partial to civil rights and has not complied with the court's time frames.

Presidential leadership is very important as it relates to the political process, and the lack of uniformity of policy in the HEW-OCR is due to politics of a particular president. The effective implementation of policy is contingent upon the successful functioning of the political process, and it is important to create the administrative capability to implement policy. Presidential leadership is one component of that process.

From the standpoint of the political process, the key question for this or any other major strategy is its acceptability to the principal partners to the process—the President, the Congress and the wide range of education constituent groups, including the recently formed client-centered groups. Assuming national concern, which is already present, acceptability, in this instance, consists of a judicious and pragmatic use of several criteria: something for everyone, reforms in behalf of equal educational opportunity, and the provision of sufficient resources overtime within budget constraints. (Hughes and Hughes, 1972, p. 193)

These ideas highlight key aspects of the political process necessary for policy implementation. Presidential leadership is identified as a key element in that process. In order to complete the political process that affects the HEW-OCR, the president must demonstrate a commitment to policy and demonstrate an investment in the budget process.

During the period 1954 to 1981, there was not a significant commitment to equal educational policy on behalf of the president. Generally, the HEW-OCR has not had a demonstrated enforcement commitment on behalf of the president (except Johnson and Carter), nor has the commitment been expressed in terms of budget appropriations. As a result, the HEW-OCR has suffered over the years from a serious lack of resources (i.e., staff, equipment, management information systems, etc.).

II. CONGRESSIONAL INITIATIVE

Just as the role of the president can affect educational policy, the actions of members of Congress can also place constraints on the administrative agency. Upon delineating certain activities of members of Congress, one can understand the effects of politics. Again, these factors reveal the lack of uniform policy enforcement in equal education matters by the Education Department, Office for Civil Rights (ED-OCR). In the House of Representatives, the committee on Education and Labor monitors and oversees issues, activities, and practices that related to educational matters. On the Senate side, the Committee on Labor and Public Welfare, through its Subcommittee on Education, monitors and oversees issues, activities, and practices that related to educational matters. Spring asserts:

> Membership in these committees is not highly prized because they deal with many highly emotional issues that have little pay-off in terms of furthering political careers. Since membership in these committees is not considered as prestigious as other committee assignments, there tends to be a high rate of turnover. Because of the lack of stability of committee membership, plus the fact that the primary interests of the committees is labor, relatively little educational expertise is to be found among committee members. (1978, p. 171)

These ideas highlight the lack of expertise found among Congressional committee members due to a lack of prestige, a high turnover rate, and an overall lack of stability.

For reasons of their own, some members of Congress challenged a Federal agency on its administrative process on a very controversial educational issue. On April 30, 1975, the Senate Subcommittee on Education held an oversight hearing on HEW enforcement of school-related civil rights problems, 1975. This hearing took place in the 94th Congress, First Session. Generally, it was an examination of the administration and enforcement of the Civil Rights

Act in elementary and secondary areas of education. Presiding was Senator J. Glenn Beall, Jr., of Maryland. The chairman of the subcommittee was Senator Claiborne Pell of Rhode Island. The hearing addressed the HEW compliance problem that affected the Anne Arundel County, Maryland, school system.

Mr. Beall cited the reasons for the hearing as follows: "The Sixth Annual Gallup Poll on public attitudes toward public education indicated that our citizens regarded lack of discipline as the No. 1 problem in 5 of the 6 years." *U.S. News and World Report* in its April 14, 1975, issue did a special report on violence in the schools:

> The second ranking problem in the Gallup survey was segregation and integration problems. So two ranking issues—discipline and discrimination—are involved here. I believe the Nation cannot and should not condone or tolerate discriminatory treatment of students. I also believe that learning cannot take place in an environment lacking reasonable discipline, and that schools and teachers cannot and should not permit discipline problems of a few students to disrupt the class or educational process of the majority. Disciplinary action can and must be administered in an even-handed manner. Justice must be colorblind in our schools as well as our society. (Hearing, Subcommittee Education Council on Public Welfare, 1975)

These ideas express segregation and integration as the second-ranking problem in the public schools but highlight disciplinary action problems as primary.

Perhaps Beall's interest also related to his home state's involvement in the dispute. Mr. Beall stated that, although the issues of discipline and discrimination were local, they had national implications. Mr. Beall also stated that the subcommittee was interested in HEW's "paper required" and "administrative burdens" that had been placed on the Anne Arundel County, Maryland, school system. Prior to the HEW-OCR response, Mr. Beall stated: "I do not believe that statistical differences in disciplinary action alone should trigger the massive fishing expedition that HEW has been conducting in Anne Arundel County" (Hearing, Subcommittee on Education, Committee in Labor and Public Welfare, United States Senate, April 30, 1975).

Bear in mind during this time frame HEW-OCR was involved in the *Adams* litigation defending the Department against the lawsuit which asserts the agency had been derelict in its duty to enforce Title VI of the Civil Rights Act.

The Subcommittee welcomed testimony from Peter E. Holmes, Director, Office for Civil Rights, Department of Health, Education, and Welfare. Mr. Holmes maintained that HEW enforces Title VI of the Civil Rights Act and that:

School districts subject to Title VI are required to submit a written assurance of compliance under which they are legally obligated to meet the requirements of Title VI and its implementing regulation.

In addition to outlining various prohibited practices and imposing certain procedural requirements, the regulation provides that school districts as well as the recipients of Federal funds, will maintain such records and submit such reports as may be necessary to ascertain compliance. (45CFR sec 806 (6) and (c))

In sum, the regulation envisions a compliance program to enforce the statute and does not impose restrictions on the areas of inquiry and scope of information which the Department may pursue in order to effectively discharge its compliance responsibility. In the elementary and secondary education area, OCR has sought to field a balanced compliance effort to deal with individual complaints and with many different but interrelated compliance problems that appear to affect large groups of students in a serious way. (Hearing, April 30, 1975)

The previous statements reveal the Department's position that the regulation does not limit the areas of inquiry and scope of information for enforcement. While HEW-OCR is being used in *Adams* for lack of enforcement, Mr. Beall and the subcommittee appear to be criticizing the Department's compliance efforts as a "fishing expedition." Mr. Beall was also contacted previously on the matter, and various communications are documented in the hearing transcripts.

Prior to the bearing Mr. Beall stated in a letter dated February 18, 1974, to Dr. Edward J Anderson, Superintendent of Schools, that he felt "concern and dismay and urged reversal of HEW's request of the school system." In addition, Senator Charles Mathias, Maryland, also assisted the local superintendent in remedying the matter with HEW-OCR by discussing the matter with agency officials. The informal political process was at work long before the actual hearing on the matter. Anderson's letter from Mathias was dated February 17, 1974, and the letter from Beall was dated February 18, 1974. The political power exerted upon the HEW-OCR by one school system superintendent is very interesting. In addition, the accusations against the department were alive prior to the fact-finding process of the investigative hearing as indicated by Mr. Beall's previous quote. In this role of the congressional committee, it is evident that the message from the "Hill" conflicted with the court's order in *Adams*. This kind of political action, the competition between competing interests groups and individuals, placed significant strain on the HEW-OCR.

Mr. Beall asserted during this hearing that Dr. Anderson, superintendent, requested help from Governor Mandel, which resulted in a state task force to look into the problem. The State Task Force found no evidence of discrimination after examining the specific charges. It was also pointed out that the initial complaints which triggered the dispute have not been validated, whereas the state task force has already found the charges in effect lacking foundation. On the local level, the school superintendent contacted every notable with power or influence to prevent the agency from exercising its enforcement responsibilities. Even prior to the investigative hearing, the presiding senator stated that the agency requirements placed a "paperwork" burden on the respondents, the Anne Arundel County, Maryland, school system. Anne Arundel County is a suburb of Washington, D.C. As the OCR investigates cases, its resources in the "pilot study" were best used in districts close to headquarters that could be monitored easily and supervised. The school system's failure to respond to requests for information regarding the allegations in the charges, while they continued to receive Federal funds places the liability on the part of the school system to absolve itself of the charges, according to law.

Mr. Holmes responded to Beall's dismay regarding the agency's practice as follows:

All four of the reviews have been initiated and only in the case of Anne Arundel County have the school officials declined to permit the office to schedule interviews with key personnel or to examine pertinent records. Specially, in Anne Arundel County, OCR was denied the right to visit selected schools and interview principals, teachers and staff, and students. (Peter Holmes' Senate Hearing Statement)

In addition, the school district had refused to provide OCR with a copy of the deputy superintendent's log of disciplinary action and

other reference to deputy superintendent's log, that log is in existence is available, and the production of it for the Federal Government in connection with this investigation would require no substantial or significant staff time on the part of local school officials.

Written instructions or policies issued by principals of various schools hearing on the policies and procedures of applying suspension, expulsion and other adverse action we understand are available and would not require substantial staff time on the part of school officials, were denied. (Senate Hearing, April 20, 1975)

These statements highlight the school system's resistance to the Department's enforcement efforts. The above scenario reveals the problems facing the OCR in carrying out its congressional mandate under the law. The compliance process in this county was wrought with delays, stall tactics, and resistance; meanwhile, taxpayers dollars (Federal financial assistance) were being used to continue the operation of the school system. Further, the OCR had to request the Department of Justice to sue the school system to secure the agency right of access to the material. The lawsuit was filed November 19, 1974, in the Federal District Court in Baltimore. On February 21, 1975, Judge Edward Northrop ruled that no Federal or state law restricts OCR's access to relevant information, even information the school system contended was confidential and not releasable.

The OCR conducted a survey of disciplinary action:

HEW's Office for Civil Rights which released the survey results yesterday did not draw any sweeping conclusions on whether they showed public school discipline was biased against blacks.

Black students, who represented 27 percent of the nearly 24 million students of all races in the 2,908 school systems, accounted for 42 percent of all suspensions and 37 percent of all expulsions.

Moreover, the HEW survey showed suspended black students missed an average of 4.5 days of school as the result of being disciplined compared to an average of 4.3 days for all minorities and only 3.5 days for white. This meant either that blacks tended to get more severe penalties, or that many were suspended more than once. (Senate Hearing document from the *Washington Post*, March 6, 1975)

These statements reveal the results of OCR's 1975 survey of disciplinary action. Given the data HEW-OCR compiled survey, it appears the OCR's practices in the Anne Arundel County, Maryland, school system were appropriate. In Anne Arundel County, Black students were approximately 3 percent of the enrollment, but approximately 27 percent of the students suspended.

In sum, various political actions and influences on the part of individuals and groups have created inconsistent policy enforcement. The HEW-OCR has had to address congressional inquiries and hearings while responding to complaints from the public as well as a lawsuit against the agency titled *Adams v. Richardson*. The members of Congress have considerable influence and control in matters involving executive branch agencies; in this instance that power and control were demonstrated in an investigative hearing regarding allegations from a constituent in a

Senator's district. Not only did two Senators get involved, but also the Government of the State, and the Secretary of the Department of Health, Education, and Welfare, Casper Weinberger.

Prior to 1970 the past practices of the Congress have dealt with education legislation in a narrow perspective. Currently, the tendency is to deal with broader issues. The Senate Select Committee on Equal Educational Opportunity since 1970 has been forging a new initiative in the definition of equality and quality.

> The Committee was given investigative rather than legislative authority in order to provide policy definitions as a foundation for future education legislation. The composition of the committee has been deliberately designed to provide a broad view of educational problems in the light of other major interest areas, and particularly the courts. The committee membership includes five members from the Senate Committee on Labor and Public Welfare, five from the Judiciary Committee, and five Senators chosen at large.
>
> Chairman Mondale's interpretation of the committee's assignment is to take a broad view of "equal educational opportunity." That is, he has refused to settle for equating equal educational opportunity either with equality of educational input resources—such as overall dollar expenditures on a per capita basis, teacher qualifications, and facilities—or with the mere exposure of the individual to an equal input of resources situation. Encompassing both of these issues, he takes the view that the broader issue of educational outcomes for the individual is the key factor. In other words, the provision of equal educational opportunity can only really be determined by what actually happens to the individual as a result of the program in the educational setting. (Hughes and Hughes, 1972, p. 201)

These ideas summarize the committee's definition of equality and quality and apply a broad interpretation to the legislation.

In the committee's first Interim Report, evidence was given that the substantive issues of equal educational opportunity would be addressed in policy formulation. The report evidenced that educational opportunity was a prime concern of the committee and that "congressional initiative" has a significant impact on policy formulation. In the case of the HEW-OCR and educational policy, congressional action is required to direct educational policy.

> As the policy-making arm of the Government the Congress ultimately decides what education programs are to be sponsored at the federal level. And as the

categorical history of USOE well attests, the Congress over the years has been particularly responsive to special needs in education. (Hughes and Hughes, 1972, p. 199)

These statements reveal Congressional action is required to direct educational policy.

The interests of Congressional committees impact the HEW-OCR officials in a variety of ways. Congressmen sometimes contact officials to ascertain policy interpretations and thrusts.

In 1967 and 1968, HEW-OCR renewed its interest in school desegregation matters due to a surge of political pressure from southern congressmen. These congressmen received pressure from constituents regarding HEW's heightened enforcement effort with southern states. The congressmen called for a balanced enforcement effort throughout the nation.

By May 1967, when Congresswoman Edith Green offered an amendment to the Elementary and Secondary Education Act requiring HEW guidelines and regulations to be uniformly applied in all regions of the country, HEW had initiated enforcement action against 259 southern school districts and had but off the federal funds of 38. The Green Amendment became law in January 1968 over the opposition of HEW, which took the position that the requirements of historically dual school systems were properly different from those with no such history and that the amendments would weaken HEW's southern enforcement by diverting needed manpower. (*Justice Delayed and Denied*, 1974)

These ideas highlight Congressional initiative and its impact on policy formulation. By April of 1968, HEW developed a separate branch to deal with northern school desegregation problems. Select staff selected special cases for Justice Department review. The HEW-OCR also opened offices in New York, Chicago, Boston, and San Francisco.

That summer, Mississippi Senator John Stennis, a member of the Senate Appropriations subcommittee having jurisdiction over HEW, added language to the pending fiscal 1969 Labor HEW appropriation bill to require HEW to assign as many staff to investigate the North as were assigned to the South. When the bill became law in October 1968, HEW had 32 staff members in the North and 67 for the South. (*Justice Delayed and Denied*, 1974, p. 12)

These statements highlight Senator John Stennis' political actions affecting HEW's enforcement policy.

In March 1969, HEW expanded its northern staff to 53, while simultaneously reducing the staff in southern states to 51. During this time, 40 school districts in 13 northern states had come under review. Of these, six districts had been sent letters of probable non-compliance. Two other school districts had been referred to the Justice Department for litigation review. Also during this period HEW began to collect enrollment data on western and northern school systems. This type of data is significant in selecting districts for compliance reviews. This type of data had traditionally been collected in southern school systems since 1966.

III. CLIENT-ORIENTED GROUPS

The second approach to viewing the effect of politics in equal education policy is from the influence groups outside of government have on the political process.

An example of political action influenced by client-centered lobbies was demonstrated by the Chicago Coordinating Council of Community Organizations (CCCO) in 1965. The CCCO federation of civil rights groups charged Superintendent of Schools Benjamin Willis was maintaining segregated vocational schools and was in collusion with the real estate board and public authorities in maintaining overcrowded, segregated schools. This example cites the beginning of political activities affecting enforcement practices.

HEW Secretary John Gardner pursued the complaint by the CCCO based on the high degree of documentation. Prior to 1965, when HEW investigators pursued the complaint, there had been a series of boycotts, lawsuits, and political confrontations. Francis Keppel, U.S. Commissioner of Education, delayed funds to the school district while the complaints were being investigated. During that time, Congress had passed the 1964 appropriations act providing Chicago with 32 million dollars. These funds were provided under the Elementary and Secondary Education Act (ESEA). Reporters at the time contended the superintendent planned to use the funds for purposes other than those intended specifically for education facility improvements at predominately white schools. It is also believed the superintendent planned to provide portable classrooms to overcrowded, predominately black high schools. The portable classrooms were called "Willis wagons."

Partly because of the racial segregation and partly because of the news of the potential misuse of the funds, Commissioner Keppel in October 1964 wrote the Illinois State Superintendent of Education that funds would be held up because the district was being put in a deferred status pending investigation of the CCCO complaint. (*Justice Delayed and Denied*, 1974, p. 9)

After this action, many political actions were at work. Superintendent Willis, Congressman Roman Pucinski, and Mayor Richard Daley collectively opposed the decision.

Superintendent Willis demanded a bill of particulars specifying what violations of Title VI were under investigation. This was a difficult demand to meet when illegal segregation in the North had not yet been defined by the courts. Representative Pucinski accused HEW of jeopardizing local control of education and threatened to bottle up further federal appropriations for public school aid. And Mayor Daley, a Democratic political power, personally met with President Lyndon Johnson requesting his assistance.

President Johnson urged HEW officials to settle the issue at once, so on October 5, only four days after the deferral letter went out, HEW negotiated a face-saving settlement, agreeing to release the funds and to withdraw HEW investiators for two months in exchange for a promise from Chicago school officials to conduct their own investigation of school zone boundaries and to reaffirm two earlier school board resolutions concerning desegregation. Morale in HEW plummeted and the Justice Department, under pressure from Illinois Senator Everett Dirksen, issued guidelines forbidding HEW to hold up funds without prior administrative hearing on the matter. (*Justice Delayed and Denied*, 1974, p. 9)

The above statements are another example which identifies political influences which effect the OCR's compliance function. The events cited reflect actions by Superintendent Willis, Congressman Roman Pucinski, and Mayor Richard Daley.

Two serious consequences faced HEW due to political forces at work during the time. First, all Title VI enforcement in the northern and western states was at a standstill for a three-year period. At the time (1965) the HEW-OCR was conducting compliance reviews in San Bernardino, San Francisco, Bakersfield, Fresno City, and Pasadena, California. In addition, reviews were underway in Wichita, Kansas, and Boston, Massachusetts. Until 1968 no effort was made to close the cases and expedite compliance.

The Office of Education explained the sluggish pace of its enforcement program by pointing out that northern school segregation was hard to establish because of the "quicksands of legal interpretation" and by asserting that OE had insufficient staff to make hard cases. Federal officials chose to let local committees deal with northern school desegregation on their own, using federal funds to finance the effort under Title IV of the 1964 Civil Rights Act, a policy which produced little desegregation . . . . (*Justice Delayed and Denied*, 1964, p. 10)

The above statements reveal the problem of legal interpretation and the lack of staff resources. These problems precluded enforcement action in the previously mentioned cities.

Another major consequence of this situation is the result of a lax enforcement effort in northern school desegregation. During 1967 and 1968, Congressional pressure reviewed HEW's interest in northern school desegregation cases. HEW officials decided to select small districts where Title VI cases could be established without a great deal of political interference. The next school districts where HEW concentrated enforcement activities were River Rouge, Ecorse, and Ferndale, Michigan, all suburbs of Detroit, Michigan. A suburb of Pittsburgh, Penn Hills Township, and Union Township were also compliance targets. HEW's activities in this regard proved less politically offensive and enhanced the department's efforts to secure compliance.

The political forces at work which were previously described provided for the beginning of HEW inconsistency of educational policy and enforcement due to politics.

A widely accepted assumption concerning HEW's laggard performance is that political shackles have been placed upon the agency by President Nixon and his chief domestic policy maker. Politics unquestionably had played an important if incalculable role. (*Justice Delayed and Denied*, 1974, p. 60)

This statement reveals that an accepted assumption is that political influences have produced HEW's poor enforcement record and politics generally has played a key role.

In the same Senate hearing previously discussed in the last section, a group named "A Coalition for Justice" testified and stated that they were a coalition of civil rights groups that came together specifically to see that the complaints of black parents in the Anne Arundel County school system would be heard.

The group's testimony provided another approach to viewing issues in the hearing: it supported the HEW-OCR position that the investigation should continue. The members—Carl Snowden, Chairperson; Samuel Gilmet; Johnie Stuble; and Glenda Neal—stated: "It is our concern that the parents, students, and other citizens in Anne Arundel County be assured of a fair investigation, that politics will non longer be used as a means to impede the investigations." The group articulated its position by citing a case study that provided evidence of the "push out" phenomenon in Anne Arundel County. The group further insisted that the parents it represents have received little effort from shcool officials to remedy complaints; therefore, government intervention is necessary. Further, the group contended:

> I would like to also note that it has been the position of the Coalition for Justice that we do not take a position on whether discrimination exists or not exists in Anne Arundel County. Our position is that a complaint has been made, and that the people, the black parents in particular, have a right to have these complaints either validated or invalidated.
>
> If HEW comes in the school system and does a thorough, judicious investigation, and out of the investigation we learn that the school district does not discriminate against blacks or other nonwhite students, then we will be happy to accept their position. (Senate Hearing, April 30, 1975)

The group's emphasis in the hearing placed concern on the HEW-OCR's role as a compliance agency. The coalition's goal was to seek Federal assistance in the matter. It is to note the group's ability to highlight politics as reason for the current lack of compliance (Hughes and Hughes, 1972, p. 209).

> Historically, the professional associations have dominated the scene of advocacy for specific education programs before incumbent administrations, as well as with the congress. In contrast, the client-oriented lobbies have often lacked the staff and sometimes the sophistication of the professional lobbies for continuous liaison on policy. 'Also, the client lobbies such as the NAACP, the Urban Coalition and the more recent Common Cause have tended to focus on the general civil rights than on education in particular. However, the situation is changing and the groups are beginning to focus on the sources of policy formulation in Washington to plead the cause of their clients within the system. (Hughes and Hughes, 1972)

These statements highlight politics as a reason for a lack of compliance. This kind of political action places pressure on the HEW-OCR to further assert the mandate given by Congress. It is not certain what form of action the agency takes; however, it does alert the government officials to the interest groups that have a stake in educational policy and enforcement.

Another form of political activity can best be described by a Mississippi group representing the Delta Ministry. This group made an impact on the Senate Committee on Public Welfare in the recitation of abuses to the ESEA Title I in June of 1969. Ruby Martin of the Washington Research Project (NAACP Legal Defense and Education Fund) was able to provide expert testimony to congressional committees on client needs and to police the administration of funds at the Federal level (Hughes and Hughes, 1972, p. 210).

The work of the Washington Research project in its review of the fiscal audits of ESEA Title I projects exposed local misuse of funds and pressed the U.S. Office of Education (USOE) to give its own public account of audit findings and returns of unused funds. In addition, the National Welfare Rights Organization had marked success in October 1973 redirecting Federal administrative policy in regard to ESEA Title I funds for clothing the poor children on the grounds that adequate clothing was necessary for student attendance (Hughes & Hughes, p. 210). This kind of political action described impacted on the HEW-USOE, and those same activities by other groups tend to explain the effect client groups can have on educational policy and legislative initiative. Just as the *amicus curiae* briefs flooded the district court during the *Adams* litigation, the efforts of client groups can change the political process.

The client-oriented groups have had an impact on court decisions and educational policy.

Signaling this trend is the newly formed National Student Lobby, which by the summer of 1972 was representing 138 schools and a constituency of one million students. Its legislative goal for 1972 was that of funding $900 million for the new basic educational opportunity grants authorized by the Education Amendments of 1972 which the lobby worked to enact. Other concerns have included civil rights, civil liberties, the war, poverty and the environment. (Hughes and Hughes, 1972, p. 211)

These statements suggest a trend in client-oriented group activity which impacts on educational policy.

This chapter delineated activities involving Federal policy in HEW during the period 1954 to 1981. The case involving the Chicago Coordinating Council Organization (CCCO) set the stage for the creation of inconsistent application of Federal civil rights policy affected by client-oriented groups. This inconsistent application of educational policy and enforcement is due to political forces at work during the times.

The political forces at work can be categorized as presidential leadership, congressional initiative, and client-oriented group activities.

CHAPTER VII

POLITICAL INTEREST GROUPS

The beginning pages of the chapter address and define "interest groups" as they are viewed in the study. The politics of Federal policy is in large measure determined by political interest groups. An organized interest group is:

> A collection of individuals that on the basis of one of more shared attitudes
> (common habits of response) make certain claims upon the other groups in the
> society for the establishment, maintenance, or enforcement of forms of behavior
> that are applied in the shared attitudes. (Truman, p. 10)

The activities of interest groups will be discussed as a factor which explains the inconsistency of educational policy and enforcement in the Department of Education.

Most interest groups reflect the viewpoints of their members; however, all members may not agree all the time. Interests sometimes lie outside of group participation. However, those who pay the cost of participation and are willing to expend resources to influence policy are given credit or the lack thereof for their activities. The simplest and most direct way to influence legislation or policy is to organize.

"Group interest" is not to be confused with organized associations. Certainly some formal organizations are part of particular interests, but no formal organization is an interest in itself. There are interests in minimum wages, higher parity for farm products, or fair trade legislation. Whoever subscribes to the values or goals of an interest or undertakes an activity in support of these goals is part of the group activity no matter to which organization he may belong (Harmon and Zeigler, 1964, p. 29).

Most organized interest groups are capable of exerting political pressure not unlike the effect of organized educational associations. Client-oriented groups also are effective in influencing agency policy as is the case with the Education Department. The analyses in this chapter will focus the effects of interest groups' ability to effect the Education Department's school desegregation enforcement effort.

Groups thus become political interest groups making their claims directly upon government or indirectly upon other groups through government. This may occur with any group, but it is especially common when the life style of group members is threatened by change. Organization of a political interest group, or a move into the political arena by an existing group created primarily for another purpose, may take place at the instigation of either a political or a nonpolitical leader.

In an increasing variety of circumstances, American government officials have also become involved in the process of negotiation among groups. This is for today not just when group to group negotiations fail, as when there is a hopeless impasse over wages between labor and management groups, but also often almost as a routine procedure whenever a group needs social change. (Adrian and Press, 1969, p. 210)

These statements explain an interest group's ability to effect policy implementation.

The study of the impact of interest groups is hard to measure. Much of the trouble lies with the data. The strength of impact generally has been measured by the activity of interest groups in state politics. Generally, this kind of analysis has measured competition rather than group effectiveness (W. Francis, 1967). It is generally difficult to measure the contribution of interest groups in public policy as well as the resolution of policy disputes. Political variables such as financial resources, malapportionment, party competition, etc., lend themselves more readily to quantification (Jennings and Zeigler, 1972).

Most analyses of interest groups focus on a single group or a single issue. In the case of the Education Department's enforcement of school desegregation policy, interest groups representation focuses on key groups or the single issue of civil rights in education. There are two major types of interest groups that are active in educational policy disputes:

First, those which have been by and large national in membership with national goals and identity; second, those organizations comprised of local offices of the national organizations dedicated primarily to local issues and local community control and development. (Perry and Feagin, 1972, p. 458)

This statement describes two major types of interest groups that are active in educational policy disputes: first, large national groups; second, local offices of national groups or local groups committed to local issues.

Recently, two teacher organizations have served as major interest groups—the National Education Association (NEA) and the American Federation of Teachers (AFA). These two groups have become involved in political activity and lobbying to gain control over American education. These groups generally are concerned with greater teacher control and participation in decision making. These groups have discussed a possible merger; and if this took place along with their support of political candidates, they could become a major political force (Spring, 1978, p. 189).

In equal education policy enforcement, teacher organizations have not played a significant role. The interest groups that have played a more significant role have been the client-oriented groups. "If one were to evaluate the overall impact of these education interest groups, one would have to consider the relationship between these groups and federal agencies as the most important" (Spring, 1978, p. 198).

Up to now, the significant role for educational interest groups has not been in influencing the passage of educational legislation as it has been in influencing the agencies which administer the legislation (Spring, 1978, p. 198). In the case of client-oriented groups, the approach has been to influence the HEW-OCR by influencing the administrative process. The lack of enforcement of the applicable civil rights laws has been the focus of client-oriented groups. Client-oriented groups place great concern on the bureaucracy.

> Governments grow ever more complex, and detail legislation has become less practicable. Thus, Congress leaves large areas of detail to administrative discretion, thus increasing the urgency with which interest groups lobby the government bureaucracy. Groups must deal with many bureaucracies in the Federal government agencies. (Adrian and Press, 1969, p. 226)

These statements highlight the concern placed on the bureaucracy by client-oriented groups.

In the case of HEW again the focus was placed on the administration to ensure compliance with equal education policy. In the area where HEW claimed "administrative discretion" in the *Adams* case, the interest groups that supported the plaintiffs wrote *amicus curiae* briefs supporting the allegations.

Interest groups can function on two levels which affect agency policies. First, groups can respond to Federal educational policy. Second, groups can pressure department officials to exert influence on policy. It is argued that the actual success of failure of policy is contingent upon the department's response to pressure or influence from groups. Despite the poor record of accomplishment of HEW there was some success.

I. INTEREST GROUP ACTIVITY ON THE LOCAL LEVEL

The Greenburgh School District No. 8 in Westchester County, New York, devoted itself so intensely to solving problems that result from deliberate integration.

The Greenburgh School District's efforts to desegregate serve as more than a model of physical desegregation; but also it moved beyond that to the reconstruction of the educational structure necessary to make the integrated situation an effective one for the black child (Buchheimer and Buchheimer; Smiley and Miller, 1968, p. 443). The negative event of the deterioration of the school system and the positive event of reconstructing the school system were important milestones in transforming a New York school district from one that was segregated and inferior to a model of integrated and quality education.

> Located about 20 miles north of New York City in prosperous Westchester County, Greenburgh District No. 8 is tied together only by its educational system. The many separate neighborhoods are not incorporated into a single political unit. There are 12,000 residents including 2,600 pupils in this five-square mile area. (Buchheimer and Buchheimer, 1968, p. 445)

These statements describe the community of Greenburgh. Between the dates 1932 and 1947, a fairly large concentration of blacks settled near the center of Greenburgh; this area was swampy with poor drainage. In 1947 Greenburgh was approximately 35 percent black, and no whites lived in the area. The school district was 90 percent black. In 1968 the population included a wide range of nationalities, religions, and races. Persons with Ph.D.s as well as executives shared the community with barely literate people and people who subsist on welfare allowances. During 1963, 42 percent of the school population was black and 58 percent of the school population was white.

The school district officials chose a plan titled the "Princeton Plan." This plan suggested that all children in grades one through three attend the all-black school and all children in grades four through six would attend the white school. A third school would continue to be a junior high for all district children. The consensus of school officials in Greenburgh argued that the plan was merely a desegregation device. They felt the "saturation" of new ideals and materials was the overriding factor in reconstructing the educational system. The school officials and parents outlined 14 different elements for success, the last element was:

> Enlightened and courageous community commitment. It was a small but active nucleus of Negro and white citizens in Greenburgh who first led the way to the

Princeton Plan and catered to voting the funds essential to carry out a sound program of integration. (Buchheimer and Buchheimer, 1968, p. 449)

These statements reveal commitment was a key element in the success of the plan.

The collection of individuals in the community, with shared attitudes and common habits or response to the establishment of an integrated quality education in the school district, accomplished their common goal of commitment is the key to the power and influence an interest group can exert.

The Greenburgh school system was not responding to a Federal desegregation order. The group acted deliberately to integrate the school system and provide quality education.

Just as pressure and influence can be exerted on the local level by interest groups, interest groups that serve to influence educational policy on the national level also are as effective. The Anti-Defamation League of B'nai B'rith, a national organization, was so interested in the Greenburgh effort the organization commissioned a study. On the national level, the interest group can exert influence based on membership size and influence.

The activities of interest groups are discussed as a factor which explains the inconsistency of educational policy and enforcement. If inconsistent educational policy and enforcement are due to politics, the activities of interest groups effect federal policy. The activities of interest groups on the national level have a greater effect on federal policy.

II. INTEREST GROUP ACTIVITY ON THE NATIONAL LEVEL

The organized group as the central feature of American political life continues to dominate pluralist thought today. According to this school American society is "fractured into congerries of hundreds of small special interest groups with incompleted overlapping membership, widely differing power exercising influence on decisions salient to them." (Polsay in Bell, Edwards, and Warner, 1969, p. 34)

These groups, while not all equally powerful, share in influencing the major decisions of government and manage to see at least some of their interests served (Davidson, 1973, p. 33).

The National Association for the Advancement of Colored People (NAACP) is the oldest and most visible civil rights organization that functions as a political interest group. The NAACP was founded in 1912 by W. E. B. Dubois, a noted black sociologist. The NAACP's major tool of influence has been its ability to press legal matters in the courts. NAACP-inspired court decisions have served to influence Federal policy in education.

> It later took the case of Herman Sweatt, a Houston mail carrier suing for entrance to the University of Texas Law School resulting in *Sweatt v. Painter* decision in 1950, an important precedent for the *Brown v. Board of Education* decision four years later. In 1956, the state attorney general, John Ben Sheppard, encouraged by Governor Allan Shivers, filed eight charges against the organization, of which the main one was barratry—the practice of soliciting lawsuits. Although the organization was enjoined from any activities other than those of an "educational and charity" nature, the outcome of the trial was considered a victory for the NAACP, as no new restrictions were placed upon it and the executive secretary of the Houston branch was not forced to make public the organization's membership roles. (Chandler and Davison, 1972, pp. 29-30)

> On January 3, 1967, Roy Wilkins reported the NAACP's gross income had increased from $1,380,313 in 1965 to $1,408,385 in 1966. He warned that the U.S. faced a prospect of frequent riots unless we launch a crash program that seriously addresses itself to gross and disgraceful racial discrimination and inequities in our public school systems in Northern and Western urban centers. (*Civil Rights*, vol. 2, 1967-68)

These statements describe NAACP activities related to federal policy. Many of the NAACP political activities have been directed through the legal defense and education fund.

On March 20, 1966, a group of 47 black business and professional men and women announced the creation of a fundraising organization known as the National Negro Business and Professional Committee for the legal defense fund. This effort sought to recruit 1,000 men and women to pledge $1,000 annual contributions to the established NAACP legal defense and education fund. The group was organized by Asa T. Spaulding, 65, of Durham, North Carolina, president of North Carolina Mutual Life Insurance Co.; and Dr. Percy L. Julian, 68, of Oak Park, Illinois, director of the Julian Research Institute. On the same date, the NAACP Legal Defense and Educational Fund appointed James M. Nabrit, 3rd, as associate counsel. Nabrit had been acting associate counsel since 1965. On March 17, he was named associate counsel of the National Office for the Rights of the Indigent, a new organization established with a one million dollar Ford Foundation grant to provide legal aid to indigents. This group was administered by the NAACP Legal Defense and Education Fund.

The fund's director-counsel, Jack Greenburg, announced June 6 a new educational project designed to inform Negroes of their rights in housing, health, employment and unemployment benefits. Jean Fairfax was appointed director of the program, called the Division of Legal Information and Community Service. It was financed by a matching $300,000 Rockefeller Foundation grant. (*Civil Rights,* vol. 2, 1967-68)

These statements identify the beginnings of the Office for the Rights of the Indigent, an arm of the Legal Defense and Education Fund.

Many of the court decisions discussed in Chapter One were brought by the NAACP Legal Defense and Educational Fund, Inc. NAACP lawyers, including current Supreme Court Justice Thurgood Marshall brought the historic *Brown v. Board of Education* case to trial. The NAACP lawyers were also instrumental in arguing the *Brown* decision. This type of political action has effected equal educational opportunity. The indirect pressure on the department comes from the court that placed orders on the administrative agency. Directly, the NAACP functions to place political pressure on the Education Department through the organization known as the Leadership Conference on Civil Rights (LCCR):

The Leadership Conference on Civil Rights, the nation's largest coalition of civil rights groups, had presented Health, Education, and Welfare Secretary John W. Gardner April 27 with a statement condemning the "slow pace" of school desegregation. Roy Wilkins, chairman of the conference, said, "The country had been misled by Southern members of Congress and Southern state and school officials into believing the guidelines are too stringent; they are not strong enough." The statement called on the department to concentrate on the "urgent problem" of *de facto* segregation. . . .

An Office of Education survey which was made public August 29, 1967, found no racial discrimination in school operations involving federal money in 3,216 of the 4,878 school districts in the 17 southern and border states that previously had used dual school systems. (The Office of Education had announced March 24 that it was ordering universities in the sports programs or forfeit federal aid). (*Civil Rights,* vol. 2, 1967-68)

The statements highlight activities of the LCCR designed to place political pressure on the Education Department..

As recently as September 16, 1981, the LCCR held an Executive Committee meeting chaired by William Taylor, Center for National Policy Review. In his absence, Ralph Neas, the Executive Director, reported that the committee would undertake a comprehensive study of the Reagan administration's performance in the area of civil rights over the last eight months.

> Ralph also presented a statement for possible adoption by the Executive Committee attacking the administration's unwillingness to enforce fully the civil rights laws of the U.S. The statement was offered in response to recent Department of Justice activities reversing long standing civil rights policies and practices in school desegregation cases. Since the Administration's actions are affecting a wide range of programs, it was additionally suggested that materials on various issues be sent out in advance of Executive Committee meetings, particularly if a statement is to be issued at the conclusion of a meeting. (Minutes, Executive Committee Meeting, September 16, 1981)

This statement describes recent LCCR activities designed to attack the administration's unwillingness to fully enforce the civil rights laws.

Benjamin L. Hooks, current LCCR chairman, is also president of the NAACP. In the same Executive Committee meeting, Hooks suggested that the committee take time to consider the serious threat of the New Right and its relevance to the LCCR. The LCCR is a coalition of 157 constituent groups. The honorary chairman of the group, Clarence M. Mitchell, Jr., was an influential partner in the deliberations on Capitol Hill during the framing of the 1964 Civil Rights Bill that became known as the 1964 Civil Rights Act. In 1964, Clarence Mitchell was president of the Washington chapter of the NAACP.

In equal education policy, the LCCR has done more than pressure Congress to enact the legislation on these matters. Just as interest groups lobby on the legislative level, lobbying on the administrative level is necessary to ensure that the "intent of Congress" is addressed in enforcement of compliance. Politics on these two levels is different; and to effectively implement a program, political action on both levels is vitally necessary.

III. THE EFFECT OF POLITICAL INTEREST GROUPS
ON DEPARTMENT OF EDUCATION OFFICE OF
CIVIL RIGHTS

Interest groups have played a significant role in Federal civil rights policy. In particular, the LCCR has spearheaded the drive for equal justice under the law. The broad-based coalition of civil rights groups maneuvered the 1964 Civil Rights Act into passage.

> Nearly 80 organizations, crossing racial, economic and religious lines, put together one of the most disciplined and effectual lobbying efforts Congressional observers have recalled. Working through the umbrella organization, the Leadership conference on Civil Rights, the lobbying group concentrated on the moral imperatives of guaranteeing equal opportunity to millions of Black Americans who had less than all privileges of citizenship. (Radin, 1977)

These statements reveal the activities of the broad-based LCCR and its effective lobbying effort.

As the 1964 Civil Rights Act moved from passage to administration, the significance the coalition placed on the act varied from title to title. Title II of the act received a great deal of congressional debate. This title of the act related to discrimination in public accommodations. While congressional debate centered on the methods of requiring access to lunch counters, swimming pools, and other public facilities, a serious implication was overlooked. Title VI required all Federal funds to be utilized in a non-discriminatory manner. This, the relationship between state and local governments, required drastic change.

The dynamics of the coalition failed to provide a body of leaders with the foreknowledge of the administrative process. In short, the expertise, dedication, and single issue (civil rights) that brought the group together failed to prove sophistication with the administration of legislation. In addition, there was limited debate in Congress affected by lobbying efforts on its part of the various interest groups in the coalition. The situation described placed a significant dilemma on the administrative process.

> On a formal level, at least, administrators had the latitiude to carry out the legislative mandate with minimal direction from Congress or the interest groups involved in the Congressional battles. The absence of extended legislative controversy created a vacuum; without specific constraints, officials could proceed with actions of their own choice. 'The government employees charged

with the implementation of title VI were given undefined discretionary authority. Although all those connected with the measure acknowledged that it was a conflict-ridden, politically sensitive issue, the dimensions of that conflict were not defined in the legislative. (Radin, 1977, pp. 146-47)

These statements reveal problems with some aspects of the administrative process. The undefined discretionary authority gave administrators additional problems.

Many bureaucrats were faced with a two-dimensional problem. First, with no direction from the Congress regarding limits or rules, the administration could view their responsibility as speaking for an unorganized body politic. With this view administrators could administer the agency with the prospect for change. Second, the situation could cause possible political embarrassment to the agency for obvious reasons.

Without rules and limits stipulated by Congress, administrators had no way to measure the potential legislative reaction and to evaluate its lasting impact on implementation attempts. in addition, administrators had no way to measure the reaction of the traditional education constituency.

Thus, the officials within HEW who sought to enforce Title VI in the education programs were faced with the challenge of devising ways to politicize their discretion—that is, to define their discretion in political terms and to use it in ways that had survival payoffs. This involved attempts to develop an active constituency—organized groups that would be attentive to the policies in relationships with Congress and providing the administrators with information. (Radin, 1977, p. 148-49)

These statements further reveal problems with the administrative process that bureaucrats faced in enforcement due to a lack of direction from Congress.

The Leadership Conference on Civil Rights (LCCR) developed a committee on compliance and enforcement. The committee was developed in May of 1966. This committee did not have its own staff and utilized loaned staff members from other committees. Due to a lack of staff, the necessary research designed to monitor compliance never took place. The preoccupation of OCCR with other legislative matters prevented the LCCR from effectively monitoring compliance with the civil rights act. The LCCR's major role is to lobby for legislation on Capitol Hill; that function of the OCCR is executed quite effectively. However, administrative lobbying is unique in that there are no clearly defined victories or defeats. The administrative process continues, and to lobby effectively requires tedious and continuous work. The LCCR also believed "executive leadership" within HEW could effectively monitor compliance. The process of calling the chief on the telephone to assert concerns regarding enforcement proved unsuccessful as a vehicle for enhanced compliance. In total, the LCCR effort to effect equal education compliance was not successful. However, other interests the LCCR has undertaken have proved more successful. It is important to note the OCCR's role is not to lobby administratively; the responsibility for administration belongs to the Education Department. The Department alone is responsible for its programs and policies.

School Desegregation Task Force. The School Desegregation Task Force was very effective in its efforts to lobby on the administrative level. The Task Force was sponsored by the American Friends Service Committee (AFSC) and the NAACP Legal Defense and Education Fund. The task force was organized to monitor 200 school districts in the south.

> Monitoring, to the Task Force, not only involved a determination of the impact of the policy, but also encompassed a serious public information effort—release of information about the policy, listing of rights of black parents, and as well, a series of state-wide meetings to explain the provisions and set up mechanisms to allow feedback from local settings. (Radin, 1970, p. 172)

These statements reveal the monitoring function was quite successful. The Task Force compiled a 59-page report titled "Implementation of Title VI of the Civil Rights Act of 1964 in Regard to School Desegregation." This report was presented to HEW Secretary Gardner (1965) at the White House Conference on Civil Rights, which shocked the administration. While only 20 people were working as volunteers, the volunteers disseminated 3,000 school desegregation kits and 85,000 copies of a brochure, "Message to Parents about Desegregating Schools." Many of the policy issues discussed in the Task Force report were discussed in a similar report by the Student Nonviolent Coordinating Committee (SNCC) report on school desegregation.

> The SNCC report cited the time lag between the policy enactment from Congress and the issuance of operational policies, the reliance on paper compliance, poor community relations, and detailed the violations and inadequacies of school officials in enforcing the policy. Because the enforcement staff was relying on paper submitted by school districts, a school district could simply certify itself by signing the 441 assurance form that said no discrimination was occurring or could submit a plan for desegregation. The detailed knowledge by Task Force members of individual district situations initially overwhelmed its OE staff. (Radin, 1977, p. 172)

These statements reveal policy issues discussed in the SNCC report on school desegregation that were similar to those discussed in the Task Force report.

This series of events began to have impact with HEW personnel. The Task Force, the Inc. Fund (NAACP Legal Defense and Educational Fund), and HEW personnel began to discuss policy issues. The effect of this activity identified key decision makers in the HEW-OCR who could be contacted, where to get information, and where to apply pressure and bring complaints. In addition, these activities brought attention to bureaucrats that a serious monitoring activity was underfoot by the Task Force as well as the Inc. Fund. The strategy of the Task Force was a "pressure strategy" placed on key policy makers and decision makers. Although the efforts were effective, oftentimes they shifted with the internal structural decisions; even so the "pressure strategy" was constant. One of the participants characterized the strategy this way:

> We accumulated complaints to show patterns of problems. We became convinced
> that the heart of the problem was that HEW had no way of finding out in a
> sustained, independent way what was going on at the school level. We felt our
> job was to provide HEW with information from the local level but to package
> it in a way in which they could see the policy implications of what they were
> doing. We had to be careful doing that—we didn't want to let the government
> cop out on its own responsibilities. To the degree that we were able to convince
> the officials of our seriousness they either took notice and acted or, at least, had
> to go through the motions of dealing with us. (Radin, 1977, p. 173)

These ideas reveal the activities involved in the Task Force "pressure strategy."

The failure to effect this strategy over a long time period proved the limit of the Task Force's impact on Federal policy. Although the activities of the Task Force reveal a small group of people with minimal resources can have a significant impact on the decision-making process in HEW.

IV. CONCLUSION

This chapter has discussed political interest group activities as they relate to Federal desegregation policy. The chapter described and delineated these activities on the local level. The Leadership Conference on Civil Rights (LCCR) played a significant role in enacting the Federal government's policies on school desegregation. The OCCR proved less effective in lobbying on the administrative level with the Education Department. Nevertheless, the LCCR is continually active in monitoring Federal desegregation and today plays a vital role as a "watchdog" for policy thrusts and initiatives. Other interest groups have played a key role in effectuating policy in the Education Department. The School Desegregation Task Force, a combined group representing the American Friends Service Committee (AFSC) and the NAACP Legal Defense and Education Fund (Inc. Fund), played vital roles using a "pressure strategy" to develop policies to enforce compliance. The Task Force was very successful in its efforts to "pressure" the administrative agency. Due to a lack of staff and resources, this small group was unable to effectuate the "pressure strategy" over a long time period. As the Title VI policy took administrative form requiring drastic changes in school districts across the country, one would expect that the requirements would generate opposition. The opposition took the form of congressional pressure as well as conflict within the administrative agency. If and when conflict was generated, the administrator needed some way of protecting himself against political reactions. The friends the administrative agency cultivated (the interest groups) help protect administrators from political "heat." However, due to the limited impact of the interest groups, the administrative agency "waivered" the storm of protest by acquiescing to the thrusts of the interest groups. Over the long period, interest group activity waned, and currently the ED-OCR is without a strong administrative lobby. The current sign of opposition to the Title VI policies is still pending in the continuing case of *Adams v. Richardson*, which has been tied up in the courts since 1973. In summary, the impact of political interest groups was very limited during the period 1954 to 1981.

> The absence of a politically connected constituency for the administrative enforcement of title VI in school matters locked in the local education administrators. They were controlled by the powers that were already influential within the established OE bureaucracy—the advocates of state control. Because it is never possible to separate implementation from legislation, the administrators were forced to appear on Capitol Hill, hat in hand to defend their activities. (Radin, 1977, p. 179)

These statements summarize the limited impact of interest group activities due to the absence of a politically connected constituency for administrative enforcement.

Therefore, the activities of political interest groups regarding federal desegregation policy failed to provide effective enforcement.

CHAPTER VIII

DISCRETIONARY EQUALITY

The preceding chapters have discussed and examined the thesis that "educational policy has been inconsistently enforced at the national level due to politics." This chapter identifies major consequences of inconsistent policy enforcement and argues that to implement equal educational opportunity, it is necessary to have uniformity of educational policy and enforcement.

New directions in the area of equal schooling can establish a coordinated Federal government approach that enforces policy in various areas (e.g., housing and employment) that effect educational opportunities.

Equal opportunity in education during the period 1954 to 1981 can be termed "discretionary equality." There are various reasons why the period is termed "discretionary equality." The reasons are: (1) the ED's administrative discretion defense in the *Adams* case, (2) a lack of coordination between branches of government, (3) a shortage of agency resources, and (4) politics. Due to these factors, "discretionary equality" exists. The issues discussed will focus on this concept of equality and justice and then give a commentary on the consequences of unequal schooling.

Admittedly policy research in social areas is only beginning; the documentation of policy development and implementation is necessary to develop better policies and effective administration. Other problems with administration are discussed in this chapter, namely, the case-by-case enforcement method, the focus on less controversial issues, and the lack of coordinated policies and practices. These problems are due to internal politics within the department and external politics between the branches of government.

I. EDUCATIONAL POLICY AND ENFORCEMENT

A review of ED's equal education enforcement efforts reveals many instances of inconsistent policy enforcement strategies in education.

Morris (1979) contends:

The record and social role of professional education provides clear evidence that higher education plays a determining role in equality of opportunity—one that reaches into all areas of life. The capacity of medical and law schools to determine which people will practice those professions is one of many examples of institutional and societal interactions and interdependence. The private power of institutions to control important social functions beyond internal academic life surfaces in their unique power to select the criteria on which the availability of physicians, lawyers, and managers to serve all America will be determined. The defects of the assumption that such decisions are "academic" and not social are illustrated by data showing the decline of black access to professional education since 1976. (p. 269)

This view, directly relates to the Department of Education's compliance and monitoring function. With much controversy around issues of inequality that relate to medical and professional schools, the Department of Education's role has been lax in enforcing Federal laws and statutes in higher education (*Federal Register*, February 15, 1978). Morris (1979) further contends:

At the same time, elements in the system, in particular the Federal government and groups of institutions, have been shown to have the pivotal capacity to improve and sustain opportunities for black Americans in higher education.

Unless we recognize the systemic nature of persistent racial inequalities, progress for blacks may never be more than marginal and episodic. Large gains have, of course, been made, but the current data show that without renewed Federal and institution commitment, we will not recoup the losses of recent years. (p. 276)

The pivotal capacity of the Department of Education's role in equal educational opportunity matters has been documented, and progress for blacks has been marginal and episodic. The major thrusts of one branch of government have been challenged by another and not enforced by another. The Supreme Court in *Brown* (1954) set the tone of the federal government's involvement in these matters. The doctrine of "separate but equal" was challenged in the Supreme Court and defeated. In the Supreme Court's opinion, the elimination of discriminatory "dual systems" in education was ordered "with all deliberate speed." Clearly, in *Brown*, the judicial branch set the tone for distinct views on these matters; and since 1954, school desegregation has been so ordered and not efficiently implemented.

In the legislative branch, many actions (which include the introduction of legislation, amendments to current law, and lobbying efforts) have been designed to render ineffective and forestall the executive branch's compliance responsibility under the Civil Rights Act of 1964. The above activities have been documented in the previous chapters. Although not all of the activities in the Congress were designed to render ineffective the compliance mechanisms in HEW, many of the concerns centered around student transportation (busing) and "racial balance." Given the moods in the country during the period 1954-1981, many changes occurred in the concept of equal opportunity. Many scholars—Moynihan (1969), Jencks (1972), and Coleman (1968)—discussed the concept of equal educational opportunity and departed from the initial meaning of access as expressed by the Supreme Court. It appeared that during the period many initiatives were afoot to "cloud" the issues and divert interests away from such a significant social problem.

The works of scholars which address the issue of race and the outcomes of schooling—Cohen, Pettigrew, and Riley (1972)—assert the issue of equal schooling became more and more complex. The authors admit the ability to pose searching questions is more highly developed than the capacity to provide solid answers. Some scholars content it is zealous to expect complete equality of opportunity in these social matters. Morris (1979) contends the situation in higher education has been highly criticized in academic circles as mentioned before, and it is not feasible to expect complete equality.

Last, the major consequences of the Department's lack of uniformity of policy and enforcement have been:

(1) The failure to implement equal educational opportunity in concert with the historic *Brown* decision

(2) The failure to implement fully the Civil Rights Act provisions which affect equal educational opportunity

(3) Ineffective school desegregation enforcement effort from 1954 to 1981

II. NEW DIRECTIONS

To date, the limits of enforcement power and the inconsistencies of ED policies and practices point out that ED has not made a firm commitment to eradicate all forms of injustice and inequality in the nation's schools. Interest group activity revealed that educational leadership in the country must take steps to develop educational systems that provide equality.

Traditionally the Federal Government has relied on educational institutions to research and develop answers to many of society's social problems. Further, research is necessary to the development of policies designed to make education equitable. The relationship has previously proved unsuccessful in the main and has escalated tensions and changed attitudes on the equality of educational opportunity (Coleman, 1966). In 1968 Coleman evaluated his report that was commissioned by the U.S. Congress and the Office of Education as follows:

> Altogether, it is clear that research to examine questions of policy can be done to provide a better base for general directions of policy. I believe Equality of Educational Opportunity has done so principally through the way in which the problem was defined, resulting in a redirection of attention from school inputs as prima facie measures of equality to school outputs, and resulting as well in an expansion of the conception of school inputs beyond those intentionally supplied by the school board. It is equally clear, however, that policy research in social areas is only beginning, and that social scientists have much to learn about how to answer policy-related questions. (p. 167)

This statement by Coleman is important in this instance, due to the current social sensitivity to the issues of equality of educational opportunity. It is hoped that this study will encourage social scientists to promote the research and development of policy-related questions. Coleman (1966) also points out that:

> More generally, it appears that the most promising possibility for policy research lies in much more systematic and careful administrative records of social institutions. These records, if they are well maintained and comparable among schools (or for other policy questions, among other institutions), would allow analyses for policy questions to be carried out regularly and at minimal cost, by local school systems, by state systems, or nationally, p. 167)

This suggestion by Coleman is appropriate in light of the current crises in education surrounding equal opportunity issues. The hard policy questions need to be researched and developed to provide the necessary leadership that educational leaders can provide in the public interest. The most promising possibility for this research lies in careful administration of records of social institutions.

Morris (1979) continues this theme by asserting that, in addition, the role the education leadership must present is that the Federal Government has a great responsibility to be accountable to the public it serves.

> The first essential component in equalizing educational opportunity is the federal government. Although it is outside the standard concept of systems in higher education, the support and influence that the federal government provides to most of higher education makes it an integral part of any change in the system. In order to sustain progress toward equal opportunity, both the legislative and administrative branches must recognize that authorization and the real distribution of federal funds occurs in the independent, private, and quasi-private centers of institutional authority. If equal opportunity for Blacks is to be developed and protected, federal guidance will be important at many levels of institutional practice. This means that a clear policy of equal opportunity should be articulated for higher education. (p. 272)

These statements discuss the leadership role in equal education the government must present to be accountable to the public it serves. Again, the support of the government is essential in meeting the needs of the majority society; however, without the help of educational leaders the policies and practices in the Education Department will not prevail.

ED's school desegregation effort, as previously documented, has failed to be responsible to the public. The appropriate policy decisions by those in key governmental leadership positions can provide "more" equality than what the past record reflects. To gain insight into ED's policy administration, the complex nature of the effective administration of regulatory statutes was discussed and revealed the issue of "broad construction" in the definition of policy parameters. However, the ED-OCR does not only suffer from the limitation of the broad construction principle, but it suffers from key policy makers who fail to initiate concerted action to bring coordinated efforts to assist in the total enforcement strategy.

Orfield (1979) discussed the notion that the trend in government is away from any coordinated action to remedy urban problems. Given the relationship between school desegregation, housing opportunities, and employment discrimination, the concept of "equal opportunity" broadly connects at least these three issues. "The popular tendency is to deny the existence of fundamental problems, to blame the cities for their own problems, and to demand that they make the necessary cuts in services" (p. 15). As Orfield (1979) assesses the Federal impact on segregation (including education), he believes the Federal establishment has supported programs to increase incidences of segregation.

The common assumption is that although the federal government historically supported segregation of American cities, it has been working actively for integration for the past decade and a half. The assumption is incorrect. Very little of the civil rights enforcement apparatus of the federal government has been devoted to integration at any time. As for the substantive programs, they are seldom weighed in terms of their impact on segregation; therefore, their contemporary effect is often unknown. There are reasons to think, however, that the net impact of some of the most important substantive programs may still be to increase segregation. (p. 15)

These statements reveal the federal government support of programs that increase segregation rather than eliminate vistages of segregation.

In school desegregation issues, it was noted that there was a great impact in the south to eliminate discriminatory "dual systems." However, in the north, the enforcement effort was nil. Orfield (1979) suggests the reason is due to the multiplicity of duties and lack of resources available to enforce the law. Additionally, agencies are crippled if the department chief and the administration do not take the necessary leadership. Orfield (1979) suggests agencies complete these duties in the following ways:

1) Avoid racial issues and concentrate on other forms of discrimination against such groups as the handicapped and senior citizens.
2) Deal with racial differences through remedies emphasizing "equality" not desegregation.
3) Pursue individual case-by-case desegregation remedies.
4) Emphasize litigation for solution of general desegregation issues.
5) Invoke fund cutoffs to force basic changes in the local community. (p. 18)

In view of these methods to enforce compliance, the ED failed to adequately and effectively regulate in the public interest. Orfield (1979) also points out that despite the lack of a coordinated effort to ensure compliance, the goals and objectives of some agencies were different; therefore, the coordination goals also require the same definition of goals and objectives.

As officials attempt to cope with discrimination problems, the emphasis on other prohibited practices has taken attention away from matters of race. As compliance is assessed in the EEOC, many of the cases which receive remedies include settlements in sex discrimination cases as opposed to race cases. In the private sector, EEOC enforces Title VII, one observer notes:

Corporate affirmative action programs have been far more productive for white women than for black men. Black women labeled "twofers" by some personnel managers because they are counted twice on government compliance reports, once as women and once as minorities, are being employed and advanced less rapidly than white women but faster than black men (Goldfarb, 1980)

This statement serves as evidence that some attention has been focused on the less controversial issues by agencies as a means of ensuring compliance and quelling public sentiment. Orfield (1979) contents:

If an agency is to be expected to take on the most difficult part of its responsibility, there must be strong administrative signals that these changes have a high priority. Without strong leadership, agencies will seldom use their increased *discretion* to choose the most high risk ventures, even though they may be decisively important in the long run.

Additionally:

Discretionary equality may manifest itself through an agency's efforts to develop equal opportunity strategies, rather than enforcing issues that are directly related to race and segregation. Albeit, the law gives broad interpretation to the applicable statutes. Also, the law is explicit in its coverage of other "protected class" members. Nevertheless, the "equal opportunity" strategy gives some "protected class" members more equality under the law than others.

The problem of Blacks and Hispanics can be analyzed either as problems of group separation and inequality in urban society or as essentially individual problems of obtaining a fair share of services and jobs from the government and government-regulated private industry. Enforcement often attempts to redistribute services and does not deal with urban segregation. There are many examples of this approach, particularly in the civil rights review of the substantive programs. HEW's massive review of New York City consisted almost entirely of gathering information about measurable inequalities in the schools, not segregation. (Orfield, 1979, p. 20)

These ideas reveal the ED's failure to use its discretion in the manner that provides enhanced enforcement. Even though the ED used its *discretion*, the *Adams* case proved the department used its discretion in the wrong way.

The case-by-case enforcement effort is popular among most agencies; however, most interest groups feel this is not an effective means of compliance. The "systemic" approach to discrimination seeks remedies for large numbers of people. In "systemic" activities (pattern and practice) lawsuits are brought often to demonstrate evidence of inequality and discrimination. Because of the ineffectiveness of the case-by-case enforcement effort, the HEW-OCR was under judicial supervision from 1973 to 1977 (HEW News, December 29, 1977).

> After all, consideration of individual cases in a court or through a court-like process within an administrative agency reflects the tradition of the legal system and incorporates many of the ideas of due process that have been seen as the essence of justice. For lawyers, who occupy many of the policy-making positions and who also have great influence in the civil rights groups, case-by-case work often seems the best way to enforce the law. It is not surprising the civil rights groups, women's groups, and others decided to sue HEW to force processing of each individual complaint within a fixed number of months. (Orfield, 1979, p. 23)

These statements reveal the case-by-case approach which precludes enforcement of "systemic" cases. Large numbers of alleged victims of discrimination are not given the full benefit of enforcement action with the case-by-case method. As controversial decisions are determined with the use of the case-by-case method, the method can forestall the time necessary to act on other cases. It would be easier for the HEW-OCR to develop cases that relate to "systems" to give large numbers of victims of discrimination the benefits from controversial decisions.

The Justice Department serves as the government's attorney and influences the interpretation of the law. Strategies under this method of compliance can assist in providing relief and remedies to parties who through no other course (e.g., private lawsuits) would or could prevail. The Justice Department's role in law-making cases can be quite similar to the agency as it relates the "broad interpretation principle," as discussed in the chapter "The Administrative Function." Orfield (1979) contends there has been little use of the law-making case method:

> The past decade has seen little use of the leading case approach. During the Nixon and Ford administrations, the Justice Department appeared in opposition to civil rights groups in many of the leading school desegregation cases and the

important housing case *Hills v. Gautreaux*. When important urban decisions, as in *Swann v. Charlotte-Mecklenburg Board of Education* and *Keyes v. School "District No. 1 of Denver, Shannon v. HUD*, and *Gautreaux* were handed down, there was little effort either to file additional cases or to build the policies into HEW and HUD administrative enforcement policy. In fact, there was continued resistance in the Executive Branch. (p. 25)

These statements reveal the limited use of the law-making case method in the ED. Even though housing issues have come out education cases, there has been little effort to file additional cases or coordinate enforcement policy..

The administrative fund cut-off is used as a tool to ensure compliance as a last resort method. This method is not widely used, but the ED-OCR has the right to employ this procedure or refer the case to the Justice Department. Generally the approach is not without its detractors. The administrative agency has much power in that it has the continuing monitoring function, which continues after the desegregation order has been handed down by a court.

> The basic problem with administrative enforcement is political. The weapon of fund cutoff almost always wounds the agency that wields it. Even though it is in the law, and the law is written to require action, fund cutoff action is seldom seen as legitimate. Both state and local governments and a great many federal officials believe that its use damages substantive programs. It very commonly produces congressional protests and damages political support for agency programs. In order for the weapon to be credible, it must be used in a visible way when local defiance continues. (Orfield, p. 27)

These statements highlight politics as a basic problem with administrative enforcement and stalls the fund cut-off method as one of last resort.

Given the lack of judicial monitoring and resources, the administrative agency, ED-OCR played a vital role in determining policy. Agency officials who are sensitive to the "political climate" regarding certain matters, failed to take vigorous action in situations where it is warranted. Due to problems of coordination between departments within an agency and coordination of the judicial, executive, and legislative branches of government, one can understand the problems that cripple and limit the agency official. Not all of the liability for the ineffective administration of the regulatory statute falls on the agency official. The "discretion" the official uses in some instances is a determination arrived at by understanding the benefits and drawbacks of a course of action.

III. CONCLUSION

The responsibility for national leadership must fall on the executive branch of government. Much of the influence necessary to effect coordination between and among administrative agencies and the branches of government must come from the executive branch of government. Without any grand strategy or plan to effect school desegregation, the ED school desegregation enforcement effort from 1954 to 1980 can be termed "discretionary equality."

> Interagency coordination is a very useful goal in enforcing desegregation requirements in urban areas. Nothing weakens support for desegregation like incoherent, strategies. On an issue where each agency feels very highly vulnerable, joint action could provide mutual support and would be more likely to lead to a local decision that accommodation was unavoidable. Such action would also aid the courts, both in removing some of the political heat and in formulating better remedies. To the extent that the federal agencies could offer choices that were less unpopular than busing, they might actually be seen in a modestly favorable light. (Orfield, 1l979, p. 43)

These ideas highlight aspects of coordination deemed useful in effecting school desegregation. The aspects of coordination identified as implemental can provide effective and enhanced enforcement.

As previous administrations during the period 1953-1981 have attempted to handle the social problem of school desegregation, not much progress has taken place. As the Department of Education expends monies to address this complex social problem, not many new and innovative plans have come about. Of course there have been some highlights, although the setbacks have been many. As viewers of the problem observe the government's leadership or lack thereof, strategies have been developed to assist in concerted Federal action. William Taylor (1979) contends:

> It would make sense to attack school and housing discrimination in a metropolitan area in the same legal proceeding. This would result in a dual remedy. School authorities would be ordered to desegregate the public schools immediately under a plan that in most instances would require substantial busing. Housing authorities would be ordered to take immediate steps to provide opportunities for non-segregated housing throughout the area. While the housing remedy would require more time (since control over housing is far more fragmented

than control over public schools and since housing solutions may require capital outlays for construction or rehabilitation), concerned parents and students would have the assurance that gradually busing would phase down as more and more school desegregation was accomplished by residential integration. (p. 47)

This view is based on the premise that much information on housing segregation is introduced in school desegregation cases, and strategies have been developed to assist in concerted federal action. Therefore, due to the government's responsibility for schools and housing, simultaneous activities could enhance compliance in both areas.

As equal opportunity in education remains "discretionary," the lack of uniformity of policy and enforcement exists. "Discretionary equality" identifies problems with ineffective enforcement and also presents alternatives for effective implementation of equal education policy.

CONCLUDING COMMENTS

This work has documented the period from 1954 to 1981 as being one of "discretionary equality." As the government has attempted to address the problems of segregated schooling, educational policy enforcement has been inconsistent.

As the politics of equal opportunity are discussed, much attention has been given to the events leading up to the government's inconsistent enforcement of equal educational policy. Generally there were social forces designed to promote social change. The government's efforts in the area were proven lax with the *Adams* litigation, and the ED-OCR was ordered to require time frames and goals to remedy their enforcement problems. The appeals court administered the agency and made decisions on the agency's proceedings. One commentator, an Intergovernmental Affairs Specialist, states, "The leadership in the country was not committed to civil rights reform, the agency was not given the resources to do its job, and one way of killing a program is not to staff it" (Art Besner interview, October 28, 1980). Commitment has not been generated to alleviate this pressing social problem. In areas where the government is committed to programs, the job gets done (i.e., NASA, the space program).

The administrative function of the Education Department was discussed, and the ED from 1954 to 1981 was handicapped from executing its responsibilities under the law. Internal politics played a significant role where the Office of the General Counsel did not cooperate with the OCR, and external politics in the Congress, specifically the Eagleton-Biden Amendment hindered the enforcement of compliance. Problems of staff resources also complicated matters. The lack of quality personnel and adequate training presented problems.

In addition, to a conservative administration under presidents Nixon and Ford, the office lacked a case management system and suffered from a lack of policy resolution and dissemination. The agency's defense to those actions was again the claim of "administrative discretion." In fact, the agency abused its discretionary authority in these matters as determined by the *Adams* litigation.

Policy enforcement and affirmative action were discussed, highlighted, and depicted the government's regulations relevant to the remediation of past discrimination. Speaking frankly, not much has been done to remedy past discrimination. Regulations and guidelines have been developed; however, enforcement was lax. Federal funds disbursed to public education systems contained contractual obligations which prescribed anti-discrimination clauses which required affirmative action goals and timetables. The Department of Education has been discussed along with the Department of Energy as well. The Senate after returning from recess, passed the Justice Department's appropriations rider. This bill precluded the Justice Department's enforcement of desegregation laws by prohibiting the ordering school busing to achieve racial balance. The amendment went further to preclude the use of busing for school desegregation even if that proved to be the only available way to correct a constitutional violation.

The politics of Federal policy have also played a significant role in the Education Department's enforcement of equal education policy. Again, presidential leadership is the key element in developing consistency of policy and enforcement. Congressional initiative and the effects of political interest groups also serve as key factors in the politics of Federal policy.

The commitment from top management in government has over the years steered away from the sensitive area of school desegregation. This lack of commitment has been demonstrated during the period 1954 to 1981. This lack of commitment has been expressed in a variety of ways. There were no provisions in 1977 for OCR to review its compliance workload, case processing, and time frames nor the numbers and types of case resolutions and settlements. For the fiscal years 1970-1976, the OCR did not know and could not ascertain some of the following information:

a. The number of complaints in different stages of the enforcement process
b. The average age of complaints
c. The portion of complaints which received on-site review
d. The number of compliance reviews broken down by the type of discrimination
e. The portion of OCR's funding aid staff resources
f. The degree of the discrimination problem that still remained

The lack of uniform guidelines and standards presented another problem. The problem centered around different divisions which had separate policies and structure. Due to a lack of commitment on the part of Executive branch decision makers, this era of "discretionary equality" prevailed. Many politicians failed to address the issue of school desegregation in political campaigns due to its unpopularity and controversy. It is difficult to get elected to public office supporting such a controversial issue. Again due to the "controversy," government leaders and bureaucrats failed to address this social concern adequately. The problems of equal education policy enforcement will be with us for quite some time. New research must develop policy alternatives to further assist in the protection of the constitutional right to an equal and quality education.

While the effects of school desegregation have become suspect, many of the programs in the OCR seem to be coming too late. With the disfavor of "busing" represented in the Congress and "appropriations riders" discussed earlier, one might wonder if the uniformity of educational policy and enforcement is currently warranted. Despite the current philosophy of the Reagan administration, which appears uncertain as it relates to civil rights, the following article appeared in the *Washington Post* on January 7, 1981:

> Terrel Bell Reported Choice To Become
> Education Secretary
> It is not clear, however, what will happen to the Education Department's civil rights division, which has been at the center of controversies over school desegregation, sex discrimination, bilingual education and opportunities for handicapped students.

This statement highlights the uncertainty of the OCR's continued existence as an effective enforcement agency.

Many blacks and minorities suspect the Republican philosophy, which traditionally does not favor social programs, will affect the current civil rights gains of the past. The article "Worry Time for Blacks," in *Newsweek*, December 1, 1980, stated:

> Even those who fear the worst take some measure of comfort from the notion that a conservative backlash might serve as a wakeup call for a disorganized and dispirited black America. Faced with cutbacks, some argue, blacks might be less prone to take past successes for granted and be more willing to re-engage in both political and grassroots action. "We're sharpening our weapons and waiting to see what happens," says M. Carl Holman of the National Urban Coalition. "We're in for some tough times, but it might just have a tonic effect."

These statements highlight the uncertainty of continued gains in civil rights enforcement. Just as the conservative tide was unpredicted, political events and social forces may have an effect on the future, that will exacerbate the quest for equal opportunity in education. Additionally, the successful results of desegregated schools will provide evidence to support more initiatives.

Lastly, "discretionary equality" describes the status of equal educational opportunity from 1954 to 1981. Certain rights of citizens guaranteed by courts and statutes during the period were not given. Although these rights are guaranteed by statute against arbitrary and oppressive conduct on the part of the state, this period of history did not provide those ideals. Certain basic social freedoms in education to which citizens have a "right" should be enjoyed. This guaranteed enjoyment is the basic content of the status of citizen. It is hoped that the future will provide these civil rights.

BIBLIOGRAPHY

1. Books, pamphlets, etc., not identified with a series:

Adrian, Charles and Press, Charles. *The American political process.* New York: McGraw-Hill, 1969.

Bell, Roderick, Edwards, David V., and Wagner, R. Harrison. *The pluralist alternative: A reader in theory and research.* New York: Free Press, 1969.

Cohen, David K., Pettigrew, Thomas F., and Riley, Robert T. *Race and outcomes of schooling. In Mostellar, Frederick and Moynihan, Daniel P. (eds.), On equality of educational opportunity.* New York: Vintage Books, 1972.

Coleman, James S. *Equality of educational opportunity.* Washington, D.C.: U.S. Government Printing Office, 1966.

Coleman, James. *The Coleman report. In Mostellar, Frederick and Moynihan, Daniel P. (eds.), On equality of educational opportunity.* New York: Vintage Books, 1972.

Davidson, Chandler. *Biracial politics: Conflict and coalition in the metropolitan south.* Baton Rouge: Louisiana State University Press, 1972.

Duberman, Lucile. *Social inequality, class and caste in America.* Philadelphia: Lippincott, 1976.

Francis, W. *Legislative issues in the fifty states: A comparative analysis.* Chicago: Rand McNally, 1967.

Glazer, Nathan. *Affirmative discrimination.* New York: Basic Books, 1978.

Hughes, John F. and Hughes, Anne O. Equal education. Terre Haute: Indiana State University Press, 1972.

Hunt, J. What you should know about educational testing. Public Affairs Pamphlet no. 378.

Jencks, Christopher. Inequality. New York: Basic Books, 1972.

Jennings, M. Kent and Zeigler, Harmon. Interest representation in school governance: People and politics in urban society. New York: Sage, 1972.

Jensen, Arthur. Bias in mental testing. New York: Free Press, 1978.

Jones, Faustine Childress. The changing mood in America: Eroding commitment? Washington, D.C.: Howard University Press, 1978.

King, Martin L., Jr. Why we can't wait. New York: Signet Books, 1963.

Koenig, Louis W. The chief executive. New York: Harcourt, Brace & World, Inc., 1968.

Lyman, Howard B. Test scores and what they mean. Englewood Cliffs, N.J.: Prentice-Hall, 1971.

Moore, William and Wagstaff, Tommie. Black education in white colleges. San Francisco: Jossey-Bass, 1974.

Morris, Lorenzo, Elusive equality. Washington, D.C.: Howard University Press, 1979.

Mosteller, Frederick and Moynihan, Daniel P. (eds.). On equality of educational opportunity. New York: Vintage Books, 1972.

Moynihan, Daniel P. Maximum feasible misunderstanding. New York: Free Press, 1969.

Moynihan, Daniel P. The Negro family: The case for national action. Washington, D.C.: U.S. Department of Labor, 1965.

Myrdal, Gunnar. An American dilemma. New York: Harper & Row, 1962.

Muse, Benjamin. *The American Negro revolution.* Bloomington, Ind.: Indiana University Press, 1968.

Muse, Benjamin. *Ten years of prelude: The story of desegregation since the Supreme Court 1954 decision.* New York: Viking Press, 1964.

Neustadt, Richard E. *Presidential power: The politics of leadership.* New York: John Wiley & Sons, 1960.

Orfield, Gary. *Federal agencies and urban segregation steps toward coordinated action: Racial segregation, two policy views.* Carnegie Council on Higher Education, 1979.

Paper, Lewis J. *The promise and the performance: The leadership of John F. Kennedy.* New York: Crown Publishers, 1972.

Perry, David C. and Feagin, Joe R. *Stereotyping in black and white: People and politics in urban society.* New York: Sage, 1972.

Price, Steven O. *Civil Rights, vol. 2.* New York: Facts on File, 1967.

Radin, Beryl A. *Implementation, change and the Federal bureaucracy: School desegregation policy in H.E.W., 1964-1968.* New York: Teachers College Press, Columbia University.

Reid, Herbert. *The ramifications of Bakke and the destiny of affirmative action, advancing equality of opportunity.* Washington, D.C.: Howard University, Institute for the Study of Education Policy, 1978.

Smiley, Marjorie B. and Miller Harry L. *Policy issues in urban education.* New York: Free Press, 1968.

Spring, Joel. *American education: An introduction to social and political aspects.* New York: Longman, Inc., 1978.

Spring, Joel. *The sorting machine: National educational policy since 1954.* New York: Longman, Inc., 1972.

Taylor, William A. *A concerted federal attack on urban segregation, a preliminary exploration: Racial segregation, two policy views. Carnegie Council on Higher Education, 1979.*

Truman, David B., *The government process. New York: Alfred A. Knopf, 1951.*

Washington, Booker T. *Up from slavery. New York: Doubleday & Co., 1901.*

Wilson, William Julius. *The declining significance of race. Chicago: University of Chicago Press, 1975.*

Zeigler, Harmon. *Interest groups in American society. Englewood Cliffs, N.J.: Prentice Hall, 1964.*

2. *Books, pamphlets, etc., identified as part of a series:*

Carnegie Council on Policy Studies in Higher Education. *July Making affirmative action work in higher education. San Francisco: Jossey-Bass, 1975.*

Center for National Policy Review. *Justice delayed and denied. Washington, D.C.: Catholic University of America, 1974.*

Southern Exposure. *Just schools. Chapel Hill, N.C.: Institute for Southern Studies, 1979.*

Southern Exposure. *The executive branch stumbles. Chapel Hill, N.C.: Institute for Southern Studies, 1979.*

3. *Specific articles in a book or other work other than a journal or newspaper:*

Buchheimer, Naomi and Buchheimer, Arnold. *Equality through education: A report on Greenburgh School District No. 8. New York: Anti-Defamation League, B'nai B'rith.*

Computing minorities. *Change. September 1972. Congressional Record. 2d sess. 95. H.5371 (daily ed.) June 13, 1977.*

Congressional Record. *2d sess. 95. H.6099 (daily ed.) June 17, 1977.*

Congressional Record. 2d sess. 95. S.16540 (daily ed.) September 23, 1975.

Congressional Record. 2d sess. 95. S.16280 (daily ed.) September 27, 1978.

Congressional Record. 2d sess. 95. S.14079 (daily ed.) August 23, 1978.

Congressional Record. 2d sess. 95. H.10793 (daily ed.) September 26, 1978.

Congressional Record. 2d sess. 95. H.6102 (daily ed.) June 17, 1977.

Congressional Record. 2d sess. 95. H.6099 (daily ed.) June 17, 1977.

Congressional Record. 2d sess. 95. S.80881 (daily ed.) June 28, 1977.

Congressional Record. 2d sess. 96. H.5839 (daily ed.) July 12, 1979.

Congressional Record. 2d sess. 96. S.10029 (daily ed.) July 20, 1979.

Congressional Record. 2d sess. 96. S.10423 (daily ed.) July 24, 1979.

Congressional Record. 2d sess. 96. S.10033 (daily ed.) July 20, 1979.

Congressional Record. 2d sess. 96. S.9959 (daily ed.) July 20, 1979

Equal Employment Opportunity Commission: The transformation of an agency. The Office of Public Affairs, Equal Employment Opportunity Commission, July 1978.

Equal Employment Opportunity Act of 1964. Public Law 92-261, approved March 24, 1972.

Goodman, William. The return to the quota system. New York Times Magazine, September 10, 1972.

Health, Education, and Welfare News, December 29, 1977.

Leadership Conference on Civil Rights, memorandum, October 10, 1980.

Memorandum from J. Stanley Pottinger, Director, Office for Civil Rights, Subject: Identification of discrimination and denial of service on the basis of national origin, May 25, 1970.

Memorandum to J. Stanley Pottinger from Roderick Potter of the Civil Rights Division, OGC: Use of automatic data processing in the investigation of the Dayton, Ohio, case, October 2, 1970.

Statement by President Nixon, White House press release, August 3, 1971.

U.S. Senate. Toward equal educational opportunity. December 31, 1972.

U.S. Senate. Committee on Labor and Public. Senate Subcommittee on Education. Hearing, April 30, 1975.

Webster's New Collegiate Dictionary. "Discretion."

Worry time for Blacks. Newsweek. January 14, 1980.

4. Federal government documents:

Affirmative action in employment in higher education. U.S. Commission on Civil Rights, pp. 180-81. September 1975.

Department of Health, Education, and Welfare. Policies on elementary and secondary school compliance with Title VII of the Civil Rights Act of 1964. 1966.

Department of Health, Education, and Welfare. Statistics of public schools advanced reports. Fall 1973.

Department of Health, Education, and Welfare. Digest of significant case-related memoranda. Office of Standards, Policy, and Research, Office for Civl Rights, vol. 1, no. 2. June and July 1979.

Federal Register, vol. 43, no. 21. February 15, 1978.

Federal Register. Adoption by four agencies of uniform guidelines on employment selection procedures, vol. 43, no. 166. August 25, 1978.

Federal Register. Griggs v. Duke Power Co., 401 U.S. 424 1971, vol. 43, no. 166. August 25, 1978.

Federal Register. Rules and regulations 58509: Nondiscrimination in federally assisted programs, vol. 44, no. 197. Department of Health, Education, and Welfare, Office of Civil Rights. October 10, 1979.

Federal Statement of Policies under Title VI of the Civil Rights Act of 1964 re Desegregation of Elementary and Secondary schools. 1965.

Select Committee on Equal Educational Opportunity. The Report of U.S. Senate S. Res 359 Toward Equal Educational Opportunity. February 19, 1970.

The Federal Civil Rights Enforcement Effort – 1974. Vol. III: To insure equal educational opportunity. U.S. Commission on Civil Rights. January 1975.

Twenty years after Brown. Report of the United States Commission on Civil Rights. 1975.

U.S. Commission on Civil Rights. Equal opportunity in suburbia. 1974.

Urban League. The state of Black America. New York: The Urban League, 1978.

5. Court cases:

Adams v. Califano, DCDC, 430 F.Supp. 118 Civil R. 5 (1977).

Adams v. Richardson, 480 F. 2d at 1164-1165 (D.C. Cir. 1973).

Adams v. Richardson, 480 F. 2d 1159 (D.C. Cir. 1973).

Alexander v. Holmes County Board, 369 U.S. 19 (1969).

Bakke v. Regents of the University of California, 553 12ed 1152 (1976).

Bakke v. Regents of the University of California, 438 U.S. 265 (1978).

Bakke v. University of California Board of Regents, 438 U.S. 268 (1978).

Bob Jones University v. Johnson, 396 F. Supp. (D.C.S.C. 1974) A'ffd per curiam, no. 74-2164 (4th Cir. May 28, 1975).

Brenden v. Independent School District 742, 447 F. 2d 1292, 1298 (8th Cir. 1973).

Briggs v. Elliott, 132 F. Supp. 776 LE. D.S.C. (1955) ID. at. 77.

Brown v. Board of Education, 347 U.S. 483 (1954).

Brown v. Board of Education, 347 U.S. 294 (1955).

Bucha v. Illinois High School Association, 351 F. Supp. 69, 74 (1972).

Dayton v. Brinkman, 45 U.S.C.W. 4910 (1977).

Gilpin v. Kansas State High School Activities Association, Inc., 377 F. Supp. 1241 (1974).

Green v. Board of Education of New Kent County, 391 U.S. 430 (1968).

Hobson v. Hansen, 269 F. Supp. 401 O.O.C. (1967).

Keyes v. School District No. 1, Denver, Colorado, 413 U.S. 189 (1973).

Kelly v. Board of Education, 170 F. cd 209, 228-29, 8th circuit (1959).

Milliken v. Bradley, 42 U.S. L.W. 5249 U.S. (July 25, 1974).

National Labor Relations Board v. Hearst Publications, 322 U.S. 111 (1944).

San Diego Building Trades Council et al. v. Garmon et al., 359 U.S. 236 243 (1959).

Steelworkers v. Weber, 443 U.S., 99 S, Ct. 2711, 61 L.E.D. (1979).

Swann v. Charlotte-Mecklenburg Board of Education, 402 U.S. (1971).

Regents of the University of California v. Bakke, 163 U.S.A. 550 (1978).

U.S. v. Jefferson County Board of Education, 372 F. 2d 836, 5th circuit (1960).

6. Journals:

Anderson, Theodore R. and Warkow, Seymour. Organization, size, and functional complexity: A study of administration in hospitals. American Sociological Review, v. 126, pp. 23-28. February 1961.

Blumrosen, Alfred W. Toward effective administration of new regulatory statutes. Administrative Law Review, v. 26, pp. 87-114, 209-37. 1977.

Clark, Kenneth B. Alternative public school systems. Harvard Education Review. Winter 1968.

Cohen, Howard. Compensation and integration Harvard Education Review. Winter 1968.

Colten, David. Policy for the public schools: Compensation and integration. Harvard Educational Review. Winter 1968.

Friedman, Murray. The new black intellectuals. Commentary, v. 69, pp. 47-52. June 1980.

Harvard Law Review. The effective limits of the administrative process: A reevaluation. V. 167, pp. 1105, 1107. 1954.

Hodgekinson, Harold. Education in 1985: a future history. Educational Record. Spring 1979.

Journal of Negro Education. Does the Negro need separate schools? July 4, 1935.

Kirp, David. The poor, the schools and equal protection. Harvard Education Review, v. 38, pp. 635-84. Fall 1968.

Pettigrew, Thomas. Race and equal educational opportunity. Harvard Education Review, v. 38, pp. 66-77. Winter 1968.

Pound, Roscoe. Common law and legislation. Harvard Law Review, v. 21, p. 383. 1908.

Robinson, Peter. The making of administrative policy: Another look at rulemaking and adjudication and administrative procedure reform. University of Pennsylvania Law Review, v. 118, pp. 538-39. 1970.

Rosenblum, Alfred. Davis on confining, structuring and checking administrative discretion. Law and Contemporary Problems, v. 37, pp. 49-51. 1972.

Stadolsky, Susan and Lesser, Gerald. Learning patterns in the disadvantaged. Harvard Education Review, v. 35, p. 507. 1967.

7. Newspapers:

Goldfarb, Robert. Black men are last. New York Times, March 14, 1980.

Washington Post, p. 1, April 20, 1980.

Washington Post, p. 9, April 20, 1980.

Washington Post, Book World, p. 1, April 20, 1980.

Washington Post, p. 1, July 3, 1980.

Washington Post, p. 1, July 13, 1980.

Washington Post, p. 1, November 9, 1980.

Washington Post, p. 1, January 7, 1981.

8. Legislation:

Civil Rights Act of 1964. Chicago: Commerce Clearing House, 1964.

Civil Rights Act of 1964, Title VI, 42 U.S.C.

Civil Rights Act of 1964, 42 U.S.C., pp. 88-352.

Civil Rights Act of 1964, Sec. 601, 602, 78 Stat. 252; 22 U.S.C. 2000d, 2000d-1.

Civil Rights Act of 1964, Sec. 602, 78 Stat. 252, 42 U.S.C. 2000d-1.

Civil Rights Act of 1964, Sec. 602, 603, 78 Stat. 252, 253, 42 U.S.C. 2000d-1, 2000d-2.

9. Unpublished materials:

Interview with Art Besner, Congressional Liaison, Department of Education, October 28, 1980.

Interview with Equal Opportunity Specialist James Jordan, Equal Employment Opportunity Commission, July 8, 1980.